"*Cuba beyond the Beach* [is to be] devoured by everyone interested in that mysterious island, and anyone else who simply enjoys a great read."

MARGARET RANDALL, AUTHOR OF *CHE ON MY MIND* AND
ONLY THE ROAD/SOLO EL CAMINO: EIGHT DECADES OF CUBAN POETRY

"*Cuba beyond the Beach* goes beyond boundaries: it's a carefully composed mixture of travel book, city memoir, and stimulating reflections on a changing Cuba. Dubinsky succeeds in weaving together her astute observations on daily life in Havana with insights from Cuban studies, politics, and culture. This blend succeeds in explaining the bizarre realities of a complicated country in a refreshing way. By bringing Cuban approaches to social problems, such as crime, income inequality, and housing, into dialogue with outside solutions Dubinsky puts things into perspective and evades the all-too-common praise or vilification of socialist Cuba. She shows us that Cuba is neither socialist utopia nor communist hell, but an incubator for ingenuity. I recommend this book to anyone who seeks to better understand this awfully charming country and its people—and actually learn something from them."

RAINER SCHULTZ, HARVARD UNIVERSITY,
DIRECTOR OF THE CONSORTIUM FOR ADVANCED STUDIES
ABROAD, CUBA DIVISION, IN HAVANA

"In *Cuba beyond the Beach* Karen Dubinsky has captured the ethos of Cuba and Cubans. This work is a *tour de force*."

DR. ALTHEA PRINCE, SOCIOLOGIST, AUTHOR OF *BEING BLACK*
AND *THE POLITICS OF BLACK WOMEN'S HAIR*

"Karen Dubinsky's portraits of life in Cuba are indeed beyond the beach and other worn caricatures. Her observations provide an immensely satisfying read and still whet the appetite for more. From the first chapter, she brings the reader into an encounter with Cuba that is fascinating, intriguing, and pulsing with the beauty of life in all its complexity."

MOLLY KANE, RESEARCHER IN RESIDENCE, UQAM-CIRDIS

"*Cuba beyond the Beach* is the perfect introduction to Cuba for travellers truly interested in seeing the island beyond the beach and beyond the clichés. Even those who have visited before will learn more about the history and present of the fascinating, vibrant, and perplexing city that is Havana."

HOPE BASTIAN, AMERICAN UNIVERSITY

"By cutting away at the debilitating romance, clichés, and dense propaganda that often characterizes narratives about Cuba, this wonderfully rich book provides the reader with a rare glimpse into a Cuba that continues to capture our imaginations, even as we somewhat nervously witness its dramatic history unfold."

DAVID AUSTIN, AUTHOR OF *FEAR OF A BLACK NATION*

CUBA BEYOND THE BEACH

STORIES OF LIFE IN HAVANA ★

KAREN DUBINSKY

BETWEEN THE LINES
TORONTO

Cuba beyond the Beach
© 2016 Karen Dubinsky

First published in 2016 by
Between the Lines
401 Richmond Street West, Studio 277
Toronto, Ontario M5V 3A8 Canada
1-800-718-7201
www.btlbooks.com

All rights reserved. No part of this publication may be photocopied, reproduced, stored in a retrieval system, or transmitted in any form or by any means, electronic, mechanical, recording, or otherwise, without the written permission of Between the Lines, or (for photocopying in Canada only) Access Copyright, 1 Yonge Street, Suite 1900, Toronto, Ontario, M5E 1E5.

Every reasonable effort has been made to identify copyright holders. Between the Lines would be pleased to have any errors or omissions brought to its attention.

LIBRARY AND ARCHIVES CANADA CATALOGUING IN PUBLICATION

Dubinsky, Karen, author
Cuba beyond the beach : stories of life in Havana / Karen Dubinsky.
Includes index.
Issued in print and electronic formats.
ISBN 978-1-77113-269-5 (paperback).–ISBN 978-1-77113-270-1 (epub).–ISBN 978-1-77113-271-8 (pdf)
1. Dubinsky, Karen–Travel–Cuba–Havana. 2. Havana (Cuba)–Description and travel. 3. Havana (Cuba)–Biography. 1. Havana (Cuba)–Social life and customs. I. Title.
F1675.3.D82 2016   972.91'2307   C2016-901831-8
                                   C2016-901832-6

Cover photo by Ivan Soca Pascual
Cover and text design by Ingrid Paulson
Printed in Canada
Second printing January 2017

We acknowledge for their financial support of our publishing activities the Government of Canada through the Canada Book Fund, the Canada Council for the Arts, which last year invested $153 million to bring the arts to Canadians throughout the country, and the Government of Ontario through the Ontario Arts Council, the Ontario Book Publishers Tax Credit program, and the Ontario Media Development Corporation.

TABLE OF CONTENTS

ix   ACKNOWLEDGEMENTS

1   INTRODUCTION: MORE THAN A BEACH, MORE THAN A REVOLUTION
         CUBANS, CANADIANS, AND AMERICANS: A PECULIAR TRIANGLE
         TELLING "THE TRUTH" ABOUT CUBA
         A CITY OF STORIES

29   ONE: *GENTE DE ZONA*: PEOPLE IN THE NEIGHBOURHOOD
         A COUNTRY OF OLD LADIES
         "THERE'S BEER AT THE HOSPITAL, BUT WHERE DID YOU GET THOSE EGGS?" OUR DAILY BREAD
         BICYCLES AND BEAUTIFUL CAKES
         PÁNFILO: THE *JAMA JAMA* GUY AS COLD WAR SUPERSTAR
         PREGONEROS: THE MUSICAL THEATRE OF THE STREET
         CERRO AND MY GAY TRADE UNION

WOMEN, MEN, AND THE EVERYDAY BATTLES OF THE STREET

THE FUTUROS COMMUNISTAS DAYCARE CENTRE AND
OTHER ANOMALIES OF CUBAN CHILDHOOD

72 **TWO: THOSE WHO DREAM WITH THEIR EARS: THE SOUND OF HAVANA**

WALKING OUT INTO THE NIGHT MUSIC: RANDOM HORNS
AND EVERYDAY REGGAETÓN

HOW CUBAN MUSIC MADE ME A BETTER HISTORIAN

INTERACTIVO AND EL BRECHT ON WEDNESDAYS

MOURNING SANTIAGO

"MUSIC IS MY WEAPON" TELMARY DÍAZ AND ROCHY AMENEIRO: TWO
POWERFUL WOMEN OF SOUND

FÁBRICA DE ARTE CUBANO

113 **THREE: LA NUEVA CUBA: LIFE IN THE NEW ECONOMY**

CHOPPED VEGETABLES, RESTAURANTS, AND OTHER SIGNS
OF A NEW MIDDLE CLASS

TECHNOLOGICAL DISOBEDIENCE AND THE
ENTREPRENEURSHIP OF THE POOR

REAL ESTATE AS MAGIC REALISM

TAXI! WHY I DON'T TALK IN CUBAN TAXIS

THE HAVANA YOU DON'T KNOW: STREET CRIME,
    CORRUPTION, AND *SOCIOLISMO*

A FEW STORIES ABOUT GARBAGE

154   **FOUR: CUBANS IN THE WORLD, THE WORLD IN CUBA**

LIFE WITHOUT THE INTERNET

THE DRAMA OF THE SUITCASES: HOW TO SMUGGLE A
    SALMON INTO HAVANA

TAKING CUBANS TO COSTCO

THE THERMOMETER THAT STRUCK UP MY MOST UNUSUAL FRIENDSHIP

LOOKING FOR THE ENEMY IN MANHATTAN: HOW MY FRIEND
    EMILIA ENDED THE COLD WAR

177   **CONCLUSION: *TODO SERÁ DISTINTO?***
    OUR UNCERTAIN FUTURES

185   NOTES

193   INDEX

ACKNOWLEDGEMENTS

Just about everyone I know in Havana made a contribution to this book, so my first thank you is to just about everyone I know in Havana. You are all in this book, and in my heart, in one way or another. Friends and family in Canada also made enormous contributions. Susan Belyea and Jordi Belyea Dubinsky lived many of these experiences with me. I am doubly blessed to share a first and a second home with such fine company. Susan Lord, my co-teacher, once remarked that Havana is just too big for one instructor. Both Queen's University in Canada and the city of Havana are rewarding workplaces (especially Havana), and I am happy to share them with her. Zaira Zarza and Freddy Monasterio helped me cross the Cuba-Canadian border, literally and imaginatively, more times than any of us can count and they remain inspiring examples of how to keep oneself in two worlds at once.

Several people read all or part of this manuscript and offered me valuable advice, reminded me of cool Havana moments I had forgotten, caught my errors, and pushed me to express myself clearly. Many thanks to Susan Belyea, Emilia Fernandez, Sean Mills, Freddy Monasterio, Susan Prentice, Xenia Reloba, Scott Rutherford, Shadi Shahkhalili, Pamela Simon, and Ruth Warner. Michael Riordan provided some much needed encouragement at a crucial moment.

I am so grateful for the opportunity to work with Between the Lines. The continued existence of an independent, opinionated, Canadian publishing house is a near miracle. Long may you continue. Thanks especially to Amanda Crocker, Marg Anne Morrison, and Robert Clarke for their keen editorial eyes. Thanks also to the tremendous production and promotion team: Renée Knapp, Matthew Adams, and Jennifer Tiberio.

Havana photographer Ivan Soca Pascual gave me access to his considerable archives for the front cover image. It is an honour to share his work with a broader audience. Thanks to Ingrid Paulson for her beautiful design.

I wrote this book in Canada and in Cuba. When I was in Canada, I would e-mail friends in Havana (those with functioning Internet connections) to confirm a detail or a street name or a translation. When I was in Havana, I was usually without easy Internet access, so I would text friends in Canada to google something for me. In this makeshift way I managed to be as accurate as possible, but if I got it wrong, it is definitely my bad.

A note about the people in this book: Some of the names are pseudonyms. Most are real. I asked permission to cite all private conversations. A portion of the proceeds from this book will go to the Queen's Overseas Student Travel Fund–The Sonia Enjamio Award, which helps Cuban students study in Canada and Canadian students study in Cuba.

CUBA BEYOND THE BEACH

INTRODUCTION

MORE THAN A BEACH, MORE THAN A REVOLUTION

Over a million Canadians travel to Cuba every year. Most of them go to the beach.

Who can argue with that? Canadian winters are harsh, Cuban beaches beautiful. After the attacks of September 11, 2001, when it seemed no one was getting on airplanes, Cuban tourist officials worried about what would become of their industry. That fall, a leading Canadian-Cuban expert reassured a group of tourist industry leaders: "Don't worry. They'll be here," he told them. "Canadians are more afraid of winter than they are of terrorists."[1]

Over a decade later the Cuban tourist industry is booming and visitors are increasing. Canada tops the list of tourist-sending nations in Cuba, followed by Germany, the UK, France, and Italy.[2] But when, on December 17, 2014, Barack Obama and Raúl Castro made their surprising declaration that they would like to try to behave normally toward each other, many tourists must have begun to wonder about how this warming trend would alter their attachment to Cuba. A cartoon in the *Globe and Mail* summed it up perfectly: David Parkins drew a Canadian enjoying an empty beach, while just behind him a tsunami of Americans was poised to overtake the uncluttered paradise. "Better make it a double," the Canadian says to the Cuban beachside waiter. The image is a great blend of friendship, arrogance, and insecurity. In Cuba, unlike almost anywhere else, northerners outside the United States can fantasize that these are *our* mojitos, waiters, and beaches.

Representatives of the US Chamber of Commerce, Jay-Z and Beyoncé, and tens of thousands of US college students passed through Havana long before Obama's surprise announcement. And shortly after "D17" (as it is now known in Cuba), everyone from Netflix to Conan O'Brien to Airbnb arrived to see (and benefit from) just what was so forbidden for fifty years. As the Americans re-assess their animosity toward Cuba since the 1959 revolution, it's a good time for others to also look again at their relationship with the place we think we know. Countless visitors have had over fifty years of person-to-person experience in and with Cuba that Americans have generally missed. It's one of the few places in the world where First World tourists can rub shoulders with each other without also bumping into (much less being swamped by) Americans. That's unusual and sometimes uncanny. It's also why people from around the world began a stampede to Cuba after December 17, 2014, to see it "before the Americans wreck it," as I have heard many declare. Americans have definitely made their absence felt in the past fifty years and that is changing. But what do the rest of us actually know about the place beyond the beach?

MORE THAN A BEACH, MORE THAN A REVOLUTION ★ 3

Globe and Mail cartoon, December 18, 2014. Courtesy of David Parkins

Cuba beyond the Beach is one part travel book, one part city memoir, and large part reflection on a changing Havana in a changing Cuba. Havana, the "Paris of the Caribbean" as it was dubbed a century ago, is the nation's soul and beating heart. It is a complicated, contradictory place, a combination of capitalism, communism, Third World, First World, and Other World, all at the same time.

It's a beautiful, wounded city. It bears many scars, a good number of them from the past fifty years of battle mode. The prominent seaside building that has functioned as a US embassy since official diplomatic relations were severed in 1961—and reopened with much fanfare in August 2015—is a great example. The area around the building has often been a constantly moving Cold War tableau, ringed with rival flags, statues, plaques, and billboards. In the George W. Bush era, this was a site of political theatre at its Cold War/War on Terror finest. Across the street Cubans erected billboards featuring the iconic Abu Ghraib torture victim, linking him—visually at least—to Miami-based, anti-Cuban terrorism. The US responded with an electronic billboard on the top floor of their building that broadcast nasty things about Cuba. Cuban authorities tried to block this with huge flags commemorating victims of US wars. Over it all presides a statue of the venerable Cuban national hero José Martí, holding a child, pointing an accusing finger at the US. Irreverent Cubans call this area, officially known as the "Anti-Imperialist Tribunal," the *protestodromo*.

All over the city signs and billboards proclaim revolutionary slogans, Che's portrait is ubiquitous, and daycare centres have names like Futuro Communistas. If all a visitor did was read the billboards or scan the official daily paper, *Granma*, she or he would certainly have the impression of Cuba as a country of single-minded, ideologically over-stimulated zealots. Ideology is indeed everywhere, and at first glance, Cuba seems to exist only in shades of black and white. But first impressions can be deceiving, and ideologies are lived by people, not billboards. This book is shaped by my experiences with a wide range of Cuban people.

Former US diplomat Wayne Smith says that Cuba is to US policy makers "as the full moon is to the werewolf," and US historian Louis Pérez terms Cuba the US's "obsessive compulsive disorder."[3] Maybe it's easier for non-Americans to avoid these Cold War stereotypes, to see beneath the surface. There is nothing thrilling, illicit, or even weird about a Canadian, for example, being in Cuba, because we've never considered it enemy territory. I've marvelled over the years as US colleagues—professors, usually fairly smart people—treat my frequent research and teaching visits to Cuba as something almost unbelievable, akin to visiting the moon or North Korea. "But how do you get there?" I am frequently asked by Americans who are completely oblivious that they are the only people who *don't* get there. As relations between the two countries open up, US visitors are excitedly placing their toes in water other visitors have been experiencing for a very long time.

Yet Canadians ought not to be too cocky about our own understanding of the place. A Cuban tour guide once confided in me that he far prefers German tourists to Canadians because Germans are generally more interested in Cuban culture; they want to visit museums and art galleries. Canadians, he said, just want to go to the beach. Canadian airline advertisements and websites often refer to their flights to the Caribbean not by cities but as "Sun Destinations," as though the nations are interchangeable and the purpose of all travel is tourism. Canadian pilots on flights to Havana almost always tell passengers to "have a great vacation" when they land, oblivious to the presence of business people, workers, Cubans returning home, students, and plenty of others among the tourists. Yet my experience in Havana has taught me that visitors, from Canada as elsewhere, have plenty of other interests in Cuba—histories, friendships, loves, ambitions, dealings both shady and legit—beyond the beach.

I started visiting Cuba in 1978, and have visited frequently since 2004, usually twice or three times a year. I also spent two six-month research periods living in Havana with my family. I had the good fortune to be there to witness the day normalization with the US began, December 17 2014. I come to Cuba as a visitor, but I am also a researcher, a teacher, and a friend of many Cubans. By training I am a Canadian historian, but in recent years I have done research in Cuba. I've written one book about Cuban child migration conflicts and another about one of Cuba's most beloved musicians. That one has given me a great view of Havana's contemporary music scene. In the midst of the US economic blockade, I would often arrive from Canada with auto parts for my landlord's car, toner for a University of Havana printer, and vitamins, medicine, chocolate, and Canadian cheddar for everyone I know (including the musicians). Once I arrived with a whole fresh salmon to share with friends for New Year's dinner. My partner Susan Belyea and I have watched our son Jordi grow up there, from barely reaching the wall of the seaside Malecón, to walking on top of it, to skateboarding beside it. He's grown up climbing sculptures in the plazas of Old Havana as though they were playground equipment, befriending lizards, and collecting stray bits of cable and wire from the street to fashion into art. Most memorable of all, we hovered over him in his hospital bed after he fell out of a tree in a park (onto cement) near our Vedado apartment, breaking both wrists. It gave us all a crash course in the much heralded Cuban medical system, but also in a system of neighbourliness I didn't know the extent of until we needed it.

For almost ten years I've brought several hundred Canadian university students along with me to learn about Cuban economic and cultural development. My co-teachers and I take them to art galleries, film schools, and medical schools, and they hear lectures from professors, curators, journalists, musicians, and filmmakers. In class they ask their Cuban teachers difficult questions and they generally receive thoughtful answers. After class, they roam around the city pretty much on their own, making new friends at the university, the seafront Malecón, and the vegetable markets. Havana permits a freedom of movement unimaginable in any other Latin American city. They discover things I don't know, like where to get seriously cheap drinks and what the local skateboarders are up to.

There are plenty of guidebooks that explain the Havana tourist route and detail the latest restaurants. These are useful, but this book is for those who want to understand how people in Havana live and what visitors might learn from that. Along the way, it is also about the potential and limitations of relationships across the multiple boundaries that separate the First and Third worlds. How *habaneros* (inhabitants of Havana) live, what they eat, where they go, what they listen to, and what they think. These are difficult to get at because people in Cuba, just like people everywhere, don't speak with one voice. (This was always one of the fallacies of us-government Cuban policy.) Foreigners shouldn't take the slogans on the billboards or the headlines in the newspapers any more seriously than many Cubans take them, which is not very. I am persuaded by those Cubans who characterize their daily reality as more *sociolismo* than *socialismo*—more a reciprocal network of favours among friends (*socios*) than an abstract state ideology (socialism). It's a system that is fascinating to see in practice.

Cubans have been formed by a society given to revolutionary hyperbole and polemical speeches. The most powerful country in the world labelled them "terrorists" and prior to that, a few decades ago, they were blamed (via the erroneously named "Cuban missile crisis") for almost blowing us all to smithereens. What does all this political drama mean in daily life?

The years I have spent in Havana have been momentous. When I lived there in 2004 Cubans were still digging themselves out from the collapse of their main trading partner, the Soviet Union, a period of extreme deprivation euphemistically named the "Special Period" that began in 1990. The crises began the slow process of economic transformation that continues today: the state is relaxing exclusive control over certain sectors of the economy, most notably in the agricultural and tourist sectors. A parallel dollar economy had been introduced in 1993, legalizing access to hard currency. In 2004, the US dollar was withdrawn from circulation and slapped with a 10 percent surcharge, and Cuba entered a period of dual official currencies. *Moneda nacional* or Cuban *pesos* (hereafter referred to as MN) are what most people earn, and are roughly worth one-twenty-fourth of the Cuban controvertible peso (hereafter referred to as CUC), which is pegged to the US dollar. Incentives for international tourism were also introduced, including the legalization of private restaurants and apartments (both initially under extremely strict conditions.) These reforms pulled Cuba out of the post-Soviet free fall, but they also exacerbated inequalities (especially by race) that were obvious in 2004 and inescapable now. In 2006, Fidel Castro announced he was temporarily stepping down in favour of his brother Raúl. In 2008, Raúl took power officially. That same year, the country suffered three hurricanes that hit the agricultural sector especially hard, the damage from which cost the country an estimated US$10 billion, or nearly one-fifth of its annual GDP.⁴ In 2010, Raúl Castro announced sweeping economic reforms. The state took a further step away from being the sole player in economic life, and new opportunities for self-employment (*cuentapropismo*) and foreign investment have been created. In 2011, a private real estate market was legalized. And the mother of all surprise announcements came in December 2014—that the US and Cuba would normalize their relations and work toward ending the US economic blockade and travel ban.

How have these and other big changes over the past decade played out on the streets and in the parks and neighbourhoods of Havana? The wisdom here is a compendium of what I've learned from Cuban people rather than Cuban politicians. I listen to music more than speeches; I watch more films than TV news. The conversations Cubans have with each other, their art, their music and other cultural forms, are intense, challenging, and smart. Opinions abound in Technicolor. The people in my Havana neighbourhood are old Communist ladies and their sceptical offspring, rock stars and peanut vendors, world famous street people, crabby store clerks, Spanish teachers, history professors, journalists, filmmakers, butchers, illegal seafood vendors, tour guides, and taxi drivers. All of them have lived this curious Cold War fault line in ways that are more complicated, subtle, funny, intelligent, poetic, tragic, and beautiful than any slogan could capture. As Cuba experiences some dramatic changes, there is much to appreciate and learn from in the unlikely world they have collectively built for themselves.

Over the past fifty years Cuba has been both isolated and cosmopolitan. It's been closed to Americans but wide open for

European tourists, African medical students, and Latin American political exiles, to take just a few examples. Zaira is a Cuban graduate student in Canada who translates for our course in Havana. She learned to speak English because her high school was located on the outskirts of Havana, next door to a farm where people came from all over the world to help with the harvest. A steady stream of solidarity visitors from Ireland, Norway, Japan, and South Africa helped perfect her English conversational skills, not to mention shape an excellent accent. The intensity of the US/Cuba relationship sometimes overshadows the multiple ties between Cuba and other parts of the world.

CUBANS, CANADIANS, AND AMERICANS: A PECULIAR TRIANGLE

I'm a Canadian, and as such I have a particular relationship to the place. Canadians and Cubans have crossed paths with each other regularly over the centuries. William Van Horne, for example, a former president of the Canadian Pacific Railway, is a familiar figure in Canada's past. He was present at the famous driving of the last spike that completed Canada's railway in 1885. (In the famous photo he's the one with the top hat who looks like a Monopoly game caricature of a capitalist.) Few know that Van Horne went on to help finance and run the Cuban Railroad Company, which connected Havana to the eastern provinces and the city of Santiago de Cuba in 1901. His observations of widespread rural poverty prompted him to offer some advice—ironic in hindsight—to the US military consul who ran Cuba when he was there in 1899. Van Horne tried to convince the US military government to enact land reform, taking untilled land away from absentee landlords and parcelling it out to Cubans. As Van Horne saw it, if more Cubans owned their own land, future social upheavals might be avoided. "In countries where the percentage of individuals holding real estate is greatest," he wrote, "conservatism prevails and insurrections are unknown."[5]

Canadian tycoon Max Aitkin (a.k.a. Lord Beaverbrook, one of the finest, or at least richest, sons of New Brunswick) also held investments in Cuban railway and banking interests. While touring the island in 1906, he encountered a number of other visiting Canadian capitalists who all, according to him, "seemed to be inclined to criticize and make fun of anything Cuban." He did not feel the same way; he was actually very fond of the place. This is how he put it: "Cuba compares favourably with Canada in every respect barring morals."[6] A backhanded compliment if ever there was one, but it set a kind of ambivalent, two-sided tone for Canadian feelings about Cuba for decades to come.

In 1945, Cuba was the first Caribbean country with which Canada established diplomatic ties. We've maintained those official ties ever since. In 1953, when Cuba's major opposition parties needed to meet safely, outside the country, to plan their strategy to topple the heavy-handed dictator Fulgencio Batista, they chose to meet at the Ritz Carleton Hotel in Montreal.[7] We reprised this discreet role in the negotiations between Cuba and the US leading up to December 17, 2014, hosting both parties, secretly, in Ottawa and Toronto. Unlike almost every other country in this hemisphere, we kept talking to each other after the 1959 Cuban revolution. (Only Mexico also retained ties with Cuba.) Despite the Cold War, we didn't see Cuba as the enemy. We didn't join the American economic blockade. If Cuba is America's wayward child, perhaps for ever-obedient Canadians, Cuba is that one bad friend you had in high school—the one you kept company with just to annoy your parents. Yet like all good children, we know our rebellion has limits. When Washington closed their embassy in 1961, they asked us to take their place spying on the Cubans and so we did. Former Canadian diplomat John W. Graham recalls that he outfitted himself in what he imagined to be "Soviet technician" attire at a Zellers store in Ottawa before he left for his posting in Havana in the early 1960s. The idea was to appear as Russian as possible once in Havana, in order to photograph Soviet trucks, tanks, and other military hardware, which were then sent via diplomatic courier to Washington.[8]

Some Canadians with sympathies toward the revolution made it their business to funnel information praising Castro's social reforms to their counterparts in the US through the 1960s. Material that couldn't be mailed directly to the US from Cuba was sent through Canada to various "Fair Play for Cuba" groups in the US. Ironically enough, at the same time, the Canadian embassy was sending Cuban periodicals they collected in Havana to Washington.[9] Prime Minister Diefenbaker rejected John F. Kennedy's demand that Canada fall into line with the US during the Missile Crisis of October 1962. Most famous, perhaps, was the 1976 visit of Pierre and Margaret Trudeau to Havana, the first visit of a NATO nation leader since Castro took power. It was a true bromance: Trudeau and Castro went fishing together. Fidel couldn't take his eyes off Margaret, and neither could most other Cubans. A Cuban friend who now lives in Canada remembers this visit, which took place during his Havana boyhood, as an inspirational moment: "All those old military men who run

Cuba drooling over the charming young Canadian prime minister's wife. We loved it. It made me want to see Canada."

There are plenty of Canadian-Cuban economic ties as well. Economic trade between Canada and Cuba runs at a rate of about $1 billion annually. Sherritt International accounts for a huge amount of that; it is Cuba's second largest foreign investor. Sherritt operates an enormous nickel mine in Moa, on the remote northeastern shore. Sherritt, whose former CEO Ian Delany is dubbed "Castro's Favourite Capitalist" in the Canadian media, also has oil and gas interests near Varadero, and their presence in Cuba was recently renewed until 2028. As one of Cuba's largest foreign investors in the world, Sherritt has come under fire from the US government, and Delany himself is forbidden entry to the US.[10] Cuba's most popular beer labels, Cristal and Bucanero, are manufactured by a joint venture owned by the Cuban government and Labatt. Canada exports machinery, auto parts, electronics, and grain, and in return Cuba sends (in addition to nickel) coffee, seafood, and, of course, cigars.

As well as political ties, investment, and trade relations, Canadians have shown interest in Cuba in countless other ways. Canadian universities helped educate a new generation of Cuban engineers through a CIDA-funded exchange program that sent Canadian professors to teach in engineering schools in Havana in the early 1970s, and also brought Cuban students to Canada for graduate training. Thousands of professionals had left the country after the revolution, so international programs like this were crucial. There are currently over twenty Canadian universities with active research or teaching ties in Cuba, and at least as many have had shared research projects with Cuban institutions in the past.[11]

14 ★

Bank of Nova Scotia
building, the corner of
O'Reilly and Cuba streets

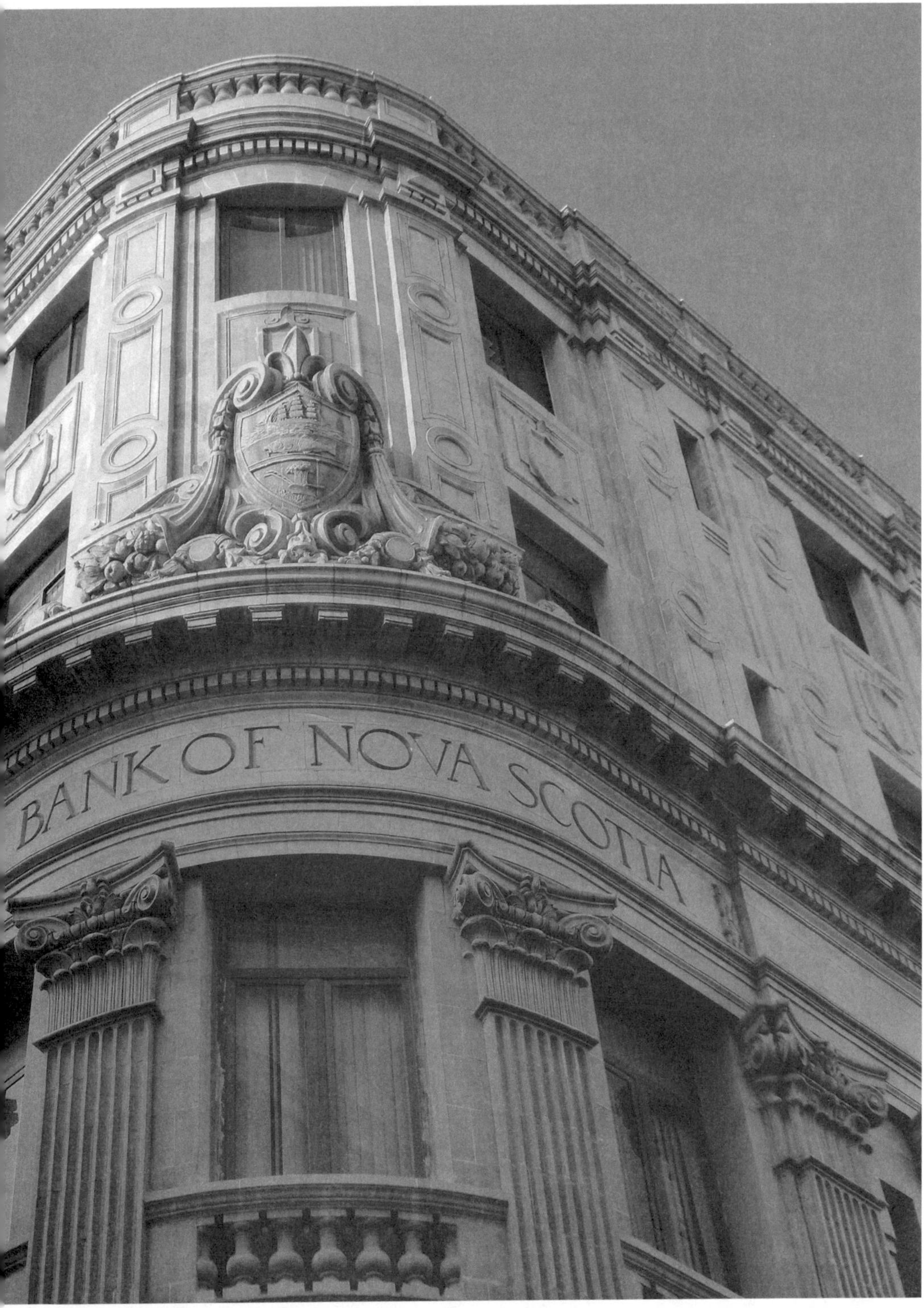
BANK OF NOVA SCOTIA

Cubans are among the few people outside Canada who know who Terry Fox is.[12] Cubans started a Terry Fox run in 1998, and it is now the largest such event outside Canada. There are plenty of other famous Canadians whom Cubans admire—Céline Dion and Justin Bieber being two celebrities Cubans seemingly can't hear enough from. One tie we'd perhaps all rather forget about is the story of James McTurk. He was convicted in Canada in 2013 of sexual crimes against children during his dozens of visits. He claimed he supported the families of his sexual partners in Cuba financially. He's the first Canadian to be convicted of child sex crimes in Cuba.

One of my favourite books about Cuban history is *On Becoming Cuban*, by the US historian Louis Pérez. It's a huge compendium of how Cuba absorbed US cultural influences for a century before the rupture of 1959. He examines everything from hairstyles to baseball to movies in order to illustrate just how saturated in things American Cuba had become prior to the 1959 revolution. Signs of Cuban/Canadian relationships are nowhere near as visible. But if you look, you can see Canada in some odd corners of Havana. Cubans dress themselves in T-shirts and ball caps from Canadian universities, sports teams, and coffee chains. I recently picked up Havana music scholar Joaquín Borges-Triana at the Toronto airport. He arrived wearing a ball cap bearing the logo of Steam Whistle, a Toronto brewery (which he had no idea was Canadian, incidentally). You can still see the chiselled name of the Bank of Nova Scotia in its old location on O'Reilly Street in Old Havana, as well as the ornate remains of the Royal Bank in Santiago de Cuba. Their buildings were quite beautiful, but Cubans didn't like Canadian banks any more than many Canadians do. Angry peasants stoned the Santiago branch in 1934, shattering its plate glass window, upset about its role in evicting five-thousand families from their homes on a sugar plantation. Over a decade later, in 1948, armed rebels trying to topple Batista assaulted the Royal Bank's Havana headquarters.[13] Despite such a mixed legacy, Canadian symbols persist. Flags and decals are ubiquitous in Havana taxis. I've watched in amazement as habaneros cart their groceries in reusable bags I barely notice in Canada: Metro, Loblaws, Canadian Tire. I once recognized a distinctive shopping bag decorated with red and white maple leaves coming toward me as I was walking along busy calle Línea in Vedado, and I was so absorbed by the sight of the bag I didn't notice the person carrying it was smiling broadly at me. She was the sister of a Cuban friend to whom I had given it a year earlier. So I have contributed my share to the symbolic Canadianization of Havana, but it works both ways. I almost benefitted directly from the generosity visiting Canadians show Cubans. In an amusing case of mistaken identity, a family of Canadian tourists, identifiable by their sunburns and Vancouver T-shirts, approached my Guatemalan-born son as we were on our way to a park in our Vedado neighbourhood. Without words, they pressed a bag of school supplies on him. We continued, confused, for a few steps until we realized they thought they were giving a donation to a Cuban kid.

TELLING "THE TRUTH" ABOUT CUBA
Cuba looms large in the imagination and fantasies of people all over the world, and getting beyond stereotypes can be a challenge. Pronouncements and photo opportunities of presidents and prime ministers are one thing; but small moments of encounter

between Cubans and non-Cubans are where the relationships really reside. The Cuban diaspora in Canada numbers about 20,000, 7,000 of whom live in Toronto. I've seen the distinctive black and orange packages of *Cubita* coffee in grocery stores in small town New Brunswick and at cigar stores in small town Ontario. There's a Cuban art gallery in Thunder Bay and Toronto now boasts a store that sells supplies for practitioners of Santaria, a traditional Afro-Cuban religion.[14] Yet we are nowhere near equal in mobility—in our access to passports, visas, or plane tickets. Owing to the lop-sided circumstances of what Eduardo Galeano calls "our upside down world," most Canadian/Cuban encounters take place on their soil. A million or so times a year.

I arrived in Cuba for the first time, along with 400 other young Canadians, for an international youth festival in 1978. I didn't know much about the place, but what twenty-one-year-old who wants to change the world could resist an opportunity to visit? The World Festival of Youth and Students invited us to celebrate, with tens of thousands of like-minded young people from around the world, "anti-imperialist solidarity, peace, and friendship." I was very young, I believed in almost everything. I was also very Canadian. It was August and I'd never experienced such heat. We spent ten heady days moving around the city from meeting to concert to art exhibition, always with too much speechifying, always on ridiculously slow buses. "Youth of the World, Cuba is Your Home" was the slogan we saw on huge billboards throughout the city. "Youth of the World, Our Buses are Your Home" was our ironic response. Despite the heat and the interminable delays, the experience was unforgettable.

Another memorable billboard lined the road on the way to the airport the day of our return home. "We will never forget you, dear and beloved friends," said huge images of Fidel Castro to thousands of impressionable young visitors. I took him at his word, and tried to make Cuba my second home. Years later, I learned that in order to make Havana more welcoming for foreigners like me, Cuban authorities had rounded up all the gay people to get them out of town for the duration. Not unlike what other governments do about other nuisances, such as poor people, during events like the Olympics. That's the Havana I've come to know: the place that embraces me even as it occasionally slaps me in the face.

X Alfonso, a popular contemporary Cuban musician, has a powerful song that lists a number of the things he hopes will change in a future Cuba. One of them is the "importance of selling an image of paradise outside."[15] He isn't just speaking of tourism. You can't blame visitors alone for acquiring superficial understandings of Cuba. Images of paradise, "sex, sun and socialism" as Jennifer Hosek terms it, have been packaged, both through tourism and political solidarity networks, to entice Europeans and North Americans for decades.[16]

Tourists are always easy to mock, and it is perhaps even easier to laugh at the naiveté of the left or liberal First World visitor in Cuba who, like me when I was twenty-one, arrives in search of a political dream. Iván de la Nuez, a Cuban writer now resident in Spain, used an image of one of Cuba's first famous leftist visitors, Jean-Paul Sartre, meeting with Che Guevera in Havana in 1960, as the cover of his book *Fantasía Rojo*. (The cover photo, like much of real life, cuts Sartre's partner Simone de Beauvoir from the photo; all you see is her foot.) *Red Fantasy* explores the Western left intelligentsia's prolonged fascination with Cuba. Both Sartre and Che are sitting, but Che looms over Sartre; his boots alone, in the foreground of the photo, are enormous. Sartre, furthermore, appears at first glance to be bowing his head. Che is actually lighting Sartre's cigar, but as de la Nuez says, "there is genuflection in Sartre's posture."[17] The dynamics of this scene — First World visitor glorifying the Cuban Revolution — have been re-enacted constantly, in some manner or other, over the past fifty years. I saw echoes of it in the T-shirt I noticed one day, worn by a visitor (blond, perhaps Canadian or maybe German) sipping a cocktail on the beautiful grounds of the Hotel Nacional, which announced "I (Heart) Fidel." That image itself evoked a line from the 2007 song *"Tercer Mundo"* (Third World) by Cuban pop group Moneda Dura. The song mocks the "proletariado de los hoteles lujosos" (proletariat of the luxury hotels) who visit Cuba with their "cameras and solidarity dollars."[18]

For decades, a steady stream of radical visitors, such as Susan Sontag, C. Wright Mills, Amiri Baraka, and Angela Davis, saw in revolutionary Cuba, to quote student radical Todd Gitlin, "everything that the US was not." Cuba was the site of what Susan Lord has termed "decolonized cosmopolitanism," in the 1960s especially, and this history of Cuba as a centre for global left-wing cultural and intellectual life is still visible all over town.[19] There are statues, plaques, and monuments to an array of important counterculture or leftist figures. The statue of John Lennon in

"For peace, bread and roses, we face the executioner." Julius and Ethel Rosenberg. Murdered June 19, 1953, at the corner of 27 and Paseo streets

POR LA PAZ EL PAN Y
LAS ROSAS ENFRENTEMOS
AL VERDUGO
ETHEL Y JULIUS ROSENBERG

ASESINADOS EL 19/6/1953

the eponymously named park is well-known, but there are plenty of others. My son used to play in a park with friends in Nuevo Vedado that featured a statue of Ho Chi Minh. There is a statue of Yasser Arafat in Miramar, a plaque to Irish martyr Bobby Sands in a park in Vedado, and my favourite, a monument to the US martyrs Ethel and Julius Rosenberg that I encountered by accident one day walking toward the National Library.

Cuba was a place to admire, to be sure, but also a place to project one's political fantasies. Today, for many outsiders the fantasy runs in reverse. Cuba is not the utopian future but rather the world we have lost. As US art critic Rachel Weiss puts it, instead of imagining Cuba as they did in the 1960s as "a place where history is being made," now for many visitors it's "the place that time forgot—Cuba as time capsule, pointed backward rather than ahead."[20]

There has been considerable genuflecting from outsiders visiting Havana over the years, just as there has been considerable condemnation. It is not just the left that sees the Cuba it wants to see; the right wing also projects their fantasies. Jeff Flake, a Republican senator from Arizona, broke ranks with his party to support Obama's new Cuba policy. As he explained to the *New York Times:* "We've got a museum of socialism 90 miles from our shore." According to him, that's something conservatives should *want* Americans to see.[21]

It is so easy to stereotype: socialist utopia or communist hell. Xenia Reloba, a writer with whom I have worked in Havana, laughs that I have been "trapped in the spider web that is our everyday reality." The spider web metaphor is more than her rhetorical flourish. I think she understands that what traps me are the infinite complex strands that hold it all in place. So rather than promising the truth, in this book I offer ambiguity, because Cuba is the most contradictory place I know.

I bring to this book the things I love and the things I hate about Havana, in the hopes that by sharing my perspective on a complicated place, visitors might, as I have, come away a little bit changed and a lot less certain. First World visitors in particular need not be blinded by ideology or guilt, which is perhaps one of the most significant things my time in Havana has taught me. I've been inspired by some beautiful writing by people who move between North America and their countries of origin in the global south: writers such as Teju Cole, Dany Laferrière, Chimamanda Ngozi Adichie, and Francisco Goldman, for example. That's not my story, but I identify with their near-permanent sense of dislocation. North Americans who undertake volunteer or solidarity work in the developing world have also influenced me. That's not my experience either, but people such as Canada's long-time African development activist, Molly Kane, have taught me plenty about the folly of believing that, as she puts it, "those who have more to give also know more."[22] In many First World/Third World encounters, it seems to me, people grapple with the same questions: what kinds of human relationships are possible in dramatically unequal circumstances? What does reciprocity mean across such formidable borders? Does money ever *not* matter? Perhaps my biggest intellectual inspiration in trying to figure out what I've learned from Cuba has come from Leela Gandhi, a theorist of post-colonial studies. She asks provocative questions about how minor but significant moments of human connection, things I describe in this book, are produced. When do small acts of friendship triumph over the overwhelming logic of global inequalities? What makes it possible to avoid the temptations of superiority that seem to arise inevitably when people are raised with plenty? I take more comfort from the possibilities I see in friendship than I do from abstract or formulaic ideology. Cuba taught me that.

There's an old joke I heard in 2004 when I spent my first extended time in Havana. It's dated and I don't think it still circulates. I recently asked my friends from whom I originally heard it to remind me of the exact wording and they had no memory of it. But for me it was a helpful introduction to Cuban complexities. A CIA agent has been in Havana for twenty years and has yet to file a report to his supervisors. They are constantly nagging him for information; finally he sends his report:

> I will never understand this country.
> There is no food in the shops, but everyone is well fed.
> There is occasionally chicken in the markets but there are never any eggs.
> The clothes in the stores are horrible but the people are beautifully dressed.
> They never finish any construction project, but no one is living on the street.
> Everyone complains about the revolution, but everyone loves Fidel.
> That's why I can't write a report about this country.

The perfect bookend to that joke is this comment I heard ten years later, when filmmaker Marilyn Solaya came to speak to our students in Havana. Solaya is a brave and talented feminist filmmaker who has made documentaries about topics like Havana's public masturbators (who, I'm sorry to inform you, you will hear more about in this book). She also just made a feature film *Vestido de Novia* (His Wedding Dress—a word play), which is about transgender issues. It won a slew of awards during the Havana film festival of 2014 and is winning awards in Europe and North America as well. Solaya is only the third woman in Cuban history to have made a feature film, and she is an unflinching critic of hypocrisy and patriarchy. When she spoke to our students she explained herself like this: "I have a conflict because I live in three countries: The country they say I live in, the country that some people live in, and the country that most people live in."

As an outsider—albeit an intimate one—in Cuba I am a part of Solaya's "the country that some people live in," the emerging dollar-and-passport-wielding middle class whom we'll hear about in this book. Solaya's "country they say I live in" is easy to spot on billboards and official media—the fantasy Cuba of slogans and pumped up ideology. It's the "country that most people live in" that I'm trying to keep in sight, and how the three countries coexist in one little island.

A CITY OF STORIES

The Spanish filmmaker Pedro Almodóvar has said that if he lived in Havana, he would simply plant a camera on a street corner and make a new film every day. This book is like Almodóvar's imaginary camera, picking up the chaotic, everyday texture of life in a confusing and wonderful place.

Havana is full of curves and alleys, and even a few dead ends, and the best stories to come out of the city, in my experience at least, are just as idiosyncratic as that human geography. On any stroll through Havana you encounter some fundamental facts and rhythms of life: The hour the little girls pour out onto the streets to head to dance class; Or when everyone heads out, grocery bags in hand, toward the bakery at virtually the same moment every day; The women and men flirting or fighting on the Malecón, Havana's living room sea wall; Apparently chaotic crowds at markets or bus stops who are actually observing a well-coordinated line-up system.

Gente de Zona is the name of a huge Cuban musical group. If you have turned on a radio in the last couple of years anywhere in the world you have probably heard them, along with Enrique Iglesias and Descemer Bueno, singing the infectiously upbeat "Bailando." *Gente de zona* translates as "people in the neighbourhood," and I think their popularity stems not only from their danceable music but also their celebration of Havana's strong neighbourhood loyalties and the range of neighbourhood characters. We'll meet a few of them here.

The sidewalks and streets of Havana are uneven and broken, as any skateboarder, wheelchair user, or baby carriage pusher can tell you. It can be a workout for the legs and feet, but when you move around Havana, you also use your ears. *Those Who Dream with Their Ears* is the name of a magazine Cuban music writer Joaquín Borges-Triana edited some years ago. (It's a bit of an inside joke, as Joaquín is blind.) He is one of the people who taught me that the sound of Havana is the key to understanding just about everything: Cuban dreams, to be sure, but also politics, history, and daily life.

Havana is changing—"renovating" in official parlance—and offering up plenty of new stories as it does. What to make of "*La Nueva Cuba*"—the new Cuba of restaurants, real estate, and market opportunities that fill the pages of North American newspapers, particularly since the Cuba/us normalization? From the streets of Havana the "New Cuba" story is contradictory and also a great deal less "new." Cubans, in their manner, have been entrepreneurial for a long time. As we'll see, the various political and economic crises of the past fifty years made Cuba an incubator for ingenuity long before the current move toward a free market.

For all the insularity of a blockaded island, Cubans do, sometimes, move around the world, virtually and otherwise. The best thing about the course I co-teach in Havana is that it is part of a reciprocal agreement: we bring students to Havana and we host Cuban academics in Canada. As a host, I have seen, up close, that Cuban journeys off the island have never been easy. But Cuban inventiveness can have a global reach and has adapted to the Internet and many other material scarcities. It also, arguably, helped to end the Cold War.

ONE

GENTE DE ZONA: PEOPLE IN THE NEIGHBOURHOOD

A COUNTRY OF OLD LADIES

The centre of my social world in Havana is a seventy-five-year-old lady. I met Vivian over a decade ago through mutual friends, when I was first looking for a place to live with my family for an extended sabbatical. Long before the Cuban government began encouraging *cuentapropismo* (self-employment), Vivian was supplementing her meagre pension from the Cuban Ministry of Finance by working as an apartment finder for foreigners. She has impeccable credentials for this position: she is a life-long Vedado resident who knows every block of the neighbourhood. Vedado isn't a tourist magnet like colonial Old Havana. But it is the centre of Cuban intellectual and cultural life: home of the University of Havana and a dozen cinemas, concert halls, and other venues. When Cubans want to describe someone with a culturally or intellectually privileged background, they refer to them as a true *"hijo de Vedado"*—a son or daughter of Vedado. It isn't the most economically fancy neighbourhood; it's not where you find the old wealth of neighbouring Miramar or even the lower density and newer dwellings of its younger sibling, Nuevo Vedado (New Vedado). But culturally, Vedado is Havana's hub. Like much of the city, Vedado's housing stock includes aging colonial elegance, 1950s modernism, and near bombed-out deterioration within the same block. Vivian's knowledge of Vedado's landlords and their housing stock was indispensable when I arrived there in 2003.

Vivian is a trim, energetic woman, with short-cropped silver hair and an easy smile. She was raised a middle-class Havana girl and so learned English in her pre-revolution Catholic private school. Unlike others of her class, her family decided to wait out the revolution, curious to see what would happen. Actually, her parents wanted to leave; Vivian convinced them to stay. She fell in love, crossing class lines, as was then the fashion, with a tobacco worker. She married the tobacco worker, the first of several husbands who came and went. A few years ago I arrived to big Vedado gossip: Vivian had a new boyfriend, though she told me recently that theirs is more of a phone relationship. Vivian loves to talk. She regularly regales me, and now my students, with stories of lining the streets of Havana to watch Fidel and company come to town in 1959. She has great tales of working at the finance ministry when Che Guevara was minister, riding the elevator with him, attending meetings with an icon my students can barely imagine as flesh and blood.

The first time we met we walked the streets of Vedado all afternoon looking at apartments together. It became legal to rent apartments to foreigners in 1993. But when I began looking ten years later, the process was still new enough that an intermediary like Vivian, an English-speaking neighbourhood lady, could carve out a little entrepreneurial niche for herself. Vivian was like an ambulatory Airbnb. She earned one dollar a day from the landlord for every client she placed. Now this niche market has been replaced by the Internet as well as an expanding Havana rental market. But that afternoon in 2003 Vivian and I went from one leafy Vedado street to another, looking at beautiful places that then cost around $25 daily. I was still learning the ropes, and was worried about whether we should be telling potential landlords that my "Canadian family" she kept referring to (to make me sound respectable, I supposed) consisted of two women and a Guatemalan adopted child, then four years old. Not so wholesomely Canadian, I feared. What would potential landlords make of same-sex parents with a kid? "Don't worry," she told me, "you aren't sex tourists who are going to fill their apartment with prostitutes. That's your trump card."

Even though nowadays the bottom has fallen out of the personal apartment-matching network, Vivian survives, although how she manages to do that is not exactly clear. She does not have family overseas who send remittances. She owns a decent, central Vedado apartment that she shares with her son and daughter-in-law. Utility charges for Havana apartments are negligible. Water and electricity are charged based on consumption, in the MN (peso) economy, and amount to pennies a month (though luxuries like air conditioners, which few have, drive the electricity bill up). Vivian and her family have fixed their apartment up to provide an unusual amount of privacy for themselves. She made a deal with a cafeteria downstairs to provide her with dinner. She doesn't have a computer or an Internet connection, but her neighbour does. So she sends and receives e-mail by simply opening her window. She teaches English classes to Cuban students, teaches Spanish to Canadian visitors—of whom she has a steady stream, and maintains a voracious interest in the world around her. We occasionally go to the movies together in December during the Havana International Film Festival. Recently we saw a documentary about the great Argentinean singer Mercedes Sosa, who lived a complicated, tumultuous life. A few days later, Vivian told me she'd heard the filmmaker, an Argentinean in town for the Havana Film Festival, interviewed on Cuban radio. There were a few points he didn't address in the on-air interview, so Vivian called him up at the radio station and chatted on the phone with him for half an hour.

This is the Vivian I adore. She feels herself to be a citizen of the world who has a perfect right to track down a visiting filmmaker at a radio station and quiz him by telephone about the finer points of his movie. (And to his credit, he responded.) She would say the revolution helped nurture this sense of intellectual curiosity, and gave her the tools to pursue her varied interests. I would say it's thanks to Vivian and the women of her generation that this place keeps hobbling along as it does. To me, she's emblematic of her generation of old *Fidelista* ladies, who have propped up this revolution—for good and for ill—for over fifty years. When Obama made his December 17, 2014, speech advocating closer US-Cuban ties, Vivian was as excited and sceptical as any Cuban I spoke to that day. "I don't trust US politicians, but really want to stay alive now," she said. She's still curious to see what will happen next.

"THERE'S BEER AT THE HOSPITAL, BUT WHERE DID YOU GET THOSE EGGS?" OUR DAILY BREAD

There's a very old joke that circulates both inside and outside Cuba which goes like this: What are the three successes of the Cuban revolution? Education, health care, and culture. What are the three failures? Breakfast, lunch, and dinner. One only has to spend a bit of time trying to feed oneself outside the tourist restaurant world to understand the truth of that joke.

For visitors, there are two kinds of grocery shopping in Havana: the market and "The Shopping." Vedado is comparatively well served by both. It houses two of the handful of supermarkets that everyone calls "The Shopping" in the city. One is located in the Galleria at Paseo, a two-storey shopping mall at the west end of Vedado, which includes a store that sells nothing but plastic flowers, several stores that sell high-end perfume and lotions, and a forlorn-looking toy store. The other Vedado supermarket is located in the FOSCSA building. This Vedado high rise, the tallest building in Cuba, looks as though it might have been a product of Soviet-era architectural brutality, but it was actually constructed a few years before the 1959 revolution. It opened its doors in 1956 as the offices of a Cuban broadcasting network, but several years later was reinvented almost completely as housing for the flood of Soviet managers and advisors who moved to Cuba in the early 1960s. The ground floor supermarket was once reserved solely for foreigners, which in those days meant mostly Soviets. Now the supermarkets are open for everyone, but the goods are sold in CUC (Cuban Convertible Pesos), equivalent to the US dollar, which few Cubans earn.

Most Cubans are paid in MN, national money or pesos. The average wage in Cuba is roughly 450–500 pesos per month, the equivalent of about $20 CUC, itself pegged to the US dollar. Some types of jobs, especially professional ones, add a further monthly bonus of $20 to $30 CUC. Pensioners generally receive around 350 pesos per month. Cuba's various social protections in the form of health care, education, and other state subsidies mean that wages mean something different; the market doesn't determine everything. That's why Cuba continues to do so well on international measures such as the United Nations Millennium Development Goals or the Human Poverty Index (in which Cuba always ranks among the top developing countries). Yet paradoxically, recent studies have concluded that almost 50 percent of the Cuban population cannot meet its basic food needs. It is not coincidental that an estimated 50 to 60 percent of the population receives remittances from relatives or friends abroad, on average $100 monthly to help with daily expenses. Some 80 percent of remittance recipients are white, which is one obvious reason for the racial visibility of economic inequality in today's Cuba. The culprit, unlike in most parts of the world, is not insufficient employment. It is insufficient wages—which is all to explain why shopping really *matters*.[1]

The supermarkets are roughly the size of a 7-Eleven or Mac's Milk in a big North American city. They smell bad and carry canned things. Some items are useful but others leave one scratching one's head: How many people would pay almost a week's salary for olives? Canned tuna, which is in demand (and both cheaper and more useful than olives), comes and goes like lightning. The supermarkets also stock frozen goods, almost none of which are useful except for the occasional chicken pieces (usually from the US) and ground turkey. Once when I was in Cuba for a long stay, I noticed that The Shopping near my house all of a sudden featured a random assortment of frozen prepared foods, such as spring rolls. I think I might have been the only one who bought them (they were horrible). The Shopping is where you find oil, crackers, cheese (one variety only), sliced meats, toilet paper, and soap. At least one-third of the store is taken up with rum, cola, and juice. One of the things I love about The Shopping is how the clerks display the single brands of olives or vinegar in rows of artful abundance, mimicking the form, if not the content, of fancy capitalist shopping. Some stores keep tins of things as common and plentiful as tomato sauce or vinegar under glass.

The market, or the agro (*agromercado*), is where you buy fruits, vegetables, and, if you have an iron will and half decent Spanish, pork. The pork comes in huge slabs that you have to negotiate down when you are a foreigner, not so much in price but in size. (Unless you want to buy a quarter of a pig at a time, which customers are encouraged to do.) When you are a foreigner, the market is also where you find people to sell you illegal things, chiefly seafood and potatoes. These products are difficult to find in the consumer market but plentiful on tables of hotels and restaurants. The young, gay, seafood vendor at my local agro greets my return to Vedado almost as enthusiastically as do my friends—though I've only ever bought one package of shrimp from him. Underground vending is tough business. Of all the tragic-comic aspects of the Cuban shopping experience, men whispering "papas" (potatoes) to you as though they were selling marijuana or porn ranks high. In the agro, you use Cuban pesos;

and the most delectable pineapple or mango will set you back less than fifty cents US.

This division between The Shopping and The Market sets the agenda for one's day. There is no such thing as a quick shopping trip. But these categorizations overlook altogether a third shopping option, not available to foreigners, which makes the Cuban shopping day even trickier. Cubans purchase their heavily subsidised food rations in state stores: *bodegas* for most items, *panaderías* (bakeries) for breads. It's a confusing system for foreigners to grasp for many reasons. *Bodegas* and *panaderías* look more like run-down government offices than grocery stores. Clerks staff the counters in front and retrieve goods for the customers. To make it more confusing, state bakeries include a *vente libre* or free sale section where non-subsidized goods are available for purchase in *moneda nacional*. There are also bakeries that sell a wider range of baked goods in CUC that aren't part of the *libreta* system. In the past, these rations included personal hygiene and cleaning products, rum, and even cigarettes. Everyone is issued a little book, the *libreta,* to keep track of their allotment. The *Libreta de Abastecimientos,* as they formally call the allotment system, was always intended as a vital supplement to the parallel market. Susan Belyea, who is writing a dissertation on how Cubans feed themselves, has been interviewing older habaneros who reminisce with great pleasure about what the *libreta* once provided: plenty of meat, beer, cigarettes, rum, and even cleaning supplies; a new broom every year. But the system has diminished so drastically in recent years that for a while there was talk of cutting it all together. The *libreta* allotment is now composed of tiny amounts of oil, rice, coffee, beans, eggs, meat, sugar, salt, and bread (with luxuries like milk, yogurt, and ground meat available for the young, the infirm, and the elderly). The *libreta* also provides one bun per day, and five eggs and a small amount of chicken or fish monthly. Years ago, as I was getting my bearings on just how Cubans acquire their daily bread, I asked a friend: Is the *libreta* enough to live on? He responded, confused at my ignorance, "You mean, for a week?" (It's a monthly ration.) Ten years later, as the state-subsidized portions shrink even further, and the coffee (for example) is replaced by a much-hated mix of coffee and dried peas, the same question would probably just provoke derision. In fact, it's now estimated that the state-subsidized *libreta* system accounts for only around 30 percent of Cubans' caloric intake. Yet the country continues to score well on global health and hunger indices, leading to one obvious conclusion: There is more than one economy.[2]

All economies have their divisions between the formal and the informal, and the Cubans hardly invented the black market. But the inconsistencies, bureaucracies, and incongruities of the Cuban system of food distribution, plus the US economic blockade, combine to produce a shopping chaos that simply boggles the mind. Items disappear and reappear with no warning or obvious pattern, and sometimes they reappear in the strangest places. One year when I was there with students, domestic beer had disappeared from virtually all the stores, but a clever student noticed a stash at a kiosk outside the hospital next to our hotel. A few years ago, coffee disappeared from The Shopping and reappeared at fancy cigar stores located in hotels. You can almost always count on getting yogurt at the liquor store in the Hotel Melia Cohiba, even when it has disappeared from The Shopping across the street. In

2011, a Chilean executive of the Rio Zaza juice processing company (Salvador Allende's former bodyguard, who had been given asylum in Cuba after the coup) was charged with various serious corruption offences. The company closed its doors. Rio Zaza held a near monopoly, so for a while there was no juice in the stores.[3]

These problems must be confronted and resolved daily, because they are endless. "*A diario, los revolucionarios*" is a popular and oft-repeated line from Havana's beloved rapper Telmary, an ironic and humorous tribute to the daily "revolutionary" acts of simple survival in Cuba.[4] The intricate reciprocities of *sociolismo* provide one solution. Friends and neighbours tell each other when items appear, or strangers ask each other on the street where they got their eggs, to take two common examples. Someone buys a large quantity of cheese and divides it among friends or neighbours, making a few *centavos* as they slice. Women separate the good grains of their rice quota from the broken, discoloured ones, and sell or trade the inferior bits to neighbours to use in desserts. Omar, an old friend who lives on a disability pension, supplements his income collecting the *libreta* quota for various neighbours, for which they pay him a tiny amount. At my Spanish teacher's house, our classes were constantly interrupted by vendors selling huge containers of products. Yogurt and chlorine were both popular. My teacher had formerly run a small restaurant and was still on the list of potential customers for the underground sales world.

The problems of food distribution create openings, both large and small, for entrepreneurship. As the *libreta* economy withers and the gap between earnings and prices expands, people appear at the market to sell not only the big-ticket items like lobster or potatoes, but also things like eggs and plastic bags. Egg purchases are conducted swiftly, one eye on the transaction, another on the crowd to spot the inspector. I now understand the caution: There was so much corruption in the egg distribution system that in 2011, eight people received harsh prison sentences (up to fifteen years) for participating in an "egg mafia"—diverting the state-run egg supply to private, black-market networks.[5] I also understand better another old Cuban joke and why egg scarcity is almost its own genre of humour: "If you want eggs, you should go to the newspaper offices to buy them, because they are always reporting on how great egg production is."

Humour is one response to problems that are obviously grave, and compounded by a frightening history: the "Special Period" of deprivation after the fall of the Soviet Union when the Cuban economy took a nosedive and daily caloric intake fell by almost 1000 calories per person. It was worse in the city; at least in the country people had the capacity to cultivate their food supply. People who survive extended periods of food insecurity tend to get extra jittery about knowing where their next meal, or shopping trip, will come from. North Americans with parents or grandparents who survived the Depression of the 1930s will recognize this condition. Almost any Cuban over the age of thirty-five probably has some memory of food deprivation, some more intense than others.

To me, this adds extra layers of poignancy to the quest for daily bread. It's a constant search, but the high points are in the early morning and late afternoon when the *bodegas* and *panadarías* are open. Havana's always lively neighbourhoods really rev up during those periods. Women predominate in the market crowds. In a study of women's daily lives in Havana in the early 2000s,

Canadian researchers Cathy Krull and Melanie Davidson asked 160 women who helped them with the household cooking, shopping, and cleaning. Some 45 percent said no one and 11 percent said their spouse helped; the rest were divided between daughters and mothers.[6] A history colleague at the University of Havana told me that one of the only good things about the Special Period was that men began to understand the value of women's domestic work. "We'd be sitting in meetings at the university," Sonia told me, "and all of a sudden someone would come in and announce that mangos were available in the market. Everyone, men and women both, would leave the meeting and run to their market to line up." Little of this rethinking of men's and women's work has stuck, though older men and the occasional younger man are visible in the crowds of people who, like clockwork, twice daily fill the streets, carrying bags or wheeling small carts. The afternoon rush, which begins around five o'clock, is my favourite time in the city. A gentle, filtered light replaces the blinding harshness of the daytime sun and, despite a long day, people become more fluid in their movements. It is crowded, but the air isn't exactly festive. Cuban shoppers are purposeful. Afternoon shopping reminds me of a song by Frank Delgado, a talented, funny chronicler of Cuban daily life. In "A Letter from a Cuban Child to Harry Potter," he scoffs at Harry Potter's magic abilities. "My mother makes magic three times a day," he sings, "to create an alchemy with only three ingredients."[7]

All of this makes the extraordinarily good dinners I have enjoyed at friends' houses in Havana even more special. A fully laid out dinner table at a Cuban home is a feast for the eyes. Salads look more like paintings or maybe mosaic sculptures: a festival of grated carrots and beets, finely sliced cucumbers, and tomatoes. The complexity of the display exists, I think, in inverse proportion to the simplicity of the ingredients. Typical Cuban specialties include black beans, fried plantain (*tostones*), and fritters (*frituras*) made from *malanga*, a root vegetable. Other vegetable delicacies are yucca (another root vegetable) drizzled with a garlic sauce, bright orange squash, and *boniato*, a sweet potato. When the Canadians visit at least, the table includes meat, usually pork or chicken, and very occasionally fish. My friends think I am being overly polite when I fill my plate with vegetable dishes and go lightly on the meat, because like poor people the world over Cubans prize meat. In truth, as good as the meat dishes are, I remain knocked out by Cuban produce because it is so ridiculously fresh. It is the original hundred-mile diet; almost no produce is imported for domestic consumption. When it is not mango season there are no mangos, period. On the rare occasion I am cooking alone, I have surveyed the contents of my fridge and, like Frank Delgado's mother, prepared an exquisite meal for myself from little more than tomatoes, onions, garlic, and *boniato*. (If I had so few ingredients in Canada this would necessitate a rush to the grocery store or a call for takeout.)

    I know the depth of the love and friendship I experience at Havana dinner tables because I understand a little of what goes on behind the scenes. The trips to the multiple markets to acquire specific ingredients, or because the yucca didn't show up in the local market that day; the line-ups; the negotiations with the neighbourhood cake lady about dessert; cleaning the little stones out of the rice or the beans; the hours spent in overheated kitchens peeling root vegetables and grating carrots. My Havana friends are always happy to receive the blockade-breaking things I bring from Canada, and we are good enough friends now that they usually ask me for things they need (at least the portable, inexpensive things). We don't do an accounting, any more than I do with friends in Canada. But even if we did, my pre-departure trips to Costco have nothing on those dinner tables.

BICYCLES AND BEAUTIFUL CAKES

I wish I had kept a list of all the things I have seen people transport on bicycles in Havana, because I am sure I have missed something. Here's what I can remember:

- several slaughtered, skinned pigs, piled on top of each other
- an enormous cake
- cans of paint
- heaping bags of flattened tin cans
- a mattress
- a dog (alive)
- a TV set
- three children (one in front, two behind)
- thirty eggs, in an open cardboard container

All of these were spectacular, but I marvel at the way Cubans transport cakes: on bicycles, on motorcycles, in buses, and of course on foot—perched, waiter-like, on one up-stretched hand, for effect. Many years ago as my kid was posing cutely in Old Havana, a random cake-carrier leaned in to photo bomb a beautiful shot. The cake was even cuter than the child. How the cakes survive excursions through Havana's heat I have long puzzled over. I'm

Cuban stranger, cake, and Canadian child, Old Havana, 2004

not fond of the taste of Cuban desserts; sweet is the overwhelming flavour of everything. But the presentation, the colours, and the reverence that goes into the making, buying, and transporting, that's worth more than the price. They look like a bridesmaid's dress: frilly and ornate, in pastel shades of pink or blue.

Maybe in a sugar economy a sweet tooth is inevitable. But I think the Cuban love of cake also stems from years of deprivation during the 1990s Special Period. Everybody has incredible Special Period survival stories, and they almost always centre on food. Sarita, a distinguished senior professor at the University of Havana, once told me her story of why she got married during the Special Period. It was one of those stories told with a practiced air; I think she tells it to everyone she meets. In Havana in

1993, everything was scarce and so everything was rationed. However, you could get permission to buy a cake for a wedding. Sarita's son's fifth birthday was coming up and she really wanted to get him a cake. So she and her partner spent two impromptu days lining up for a wedding licence, and organizing a quick ceremony so she could show up at the bakery, wedding licence in hand, to get a cake for her child. The punch line was that it tasted horrible. But it looked like a proper Cuban cake.

PÁNFILO: THE *JAMA JAMA* GUY AS COLD WAR SUPERSTAR

In the fall of 2009, Vilma, my Spanish teacher who had just moved to Canada from Cuba, decided to use short clips from YouTube to help Susan and me step up our Cuban street Spanish. She randomly selected a clip that had become popular, an Afro-Cuban guy wandering down a Havana street, ranting about food (*jama* in the vernacular). But this wasn't just any Havana street; this was the neighbourhood I've been staying in for years. The guy on the screen is ranting right in front of the vegetable market beside the apartment we usually rent. And it isn't just any random Cuban guy; it's Pánfilo.

To over one million (and counting) YouTube viewers, Pánfilo's one-minute video became a symbol of the sorry state of the Cuban economy. He sees a camera and wanders into an interview on the street. A US crew is filming a documentary about Cuban reggaetón. He interrupts. He begins yelling, saying the word *jama* repeatedly. Everyone is starving here, he yells; there is no food in Cuba. He emphasizes by gesturing, putting his hands in his empty, open mouth. Then he wanders off, stumbling as he goes.

I've seen Pánfilo (a nickname he shares with a popular Cuban comedian) wander drunk down the street plenty of times. I've heard his distinctive voice, raspy and loud, from my third floor balcony. I've learned how to avoid him when I'm on my way home, though he appears more annoying than dangerous. Sometimes he pees in public, but so do lots of Cuban males, probably not all of them drunk.

The *jama jama* video was posted on YouTube and went viral. Why is Pánfilo all of a sudden a star? What makes him different from any other drunken guy wandering and ranting down any street, any place? To some extent, old-style racism accounts for this instant popularity: there is an air of the old black minstrel show in his performance. But, once again, the shadow of the Cold War is always present, ultimately, in just about everything that happens in Cuba. The Cuban authorities arrested him for delinquency. "Free Pánfilo" groups were organized in Miami (known as *Jama y Libertad*, Food and Freedom). A Florida human rights organization adopted him as a prisoner of conscience.

Less widely reported was how Cubans in Cuba also protested: when he was arrested, his neighbours flocked to the police station to demand his release. The incarceration, according to friends in the neighbourhood, turned into a month-long hospital stay to treat his alcoholism. Soon he was back, living with his mother and annoying the neighbours once again. He still occasionally replays what I think of as Pánfilo's Greatest Hits, randomly yelling *"jama jama"* as he stumbles down the streets. Not many pay him much attention, though in 2014 another YouTube video appeared, of Pánfilo playing Pánfilo, reprising the original—ironically, I think. Even more recently, "Pánfilo's wife" has had a few moments of YouTube fame.

One day, about a year after his YouTube debut, I was in Havana, heading home with a Cuban friend, when I saw Pánfilo approaching. I made my customary plan about where to walk to avoid him. My friend Emilia headed straight for him and they embraced. She doesn't call him Pánfilo, she calls him by his name. They are old friends. He was her math professor at the University of Havana.

PREGONEROS: THE MUSICAL THEATRE OF THE STREET

Pregoneros are the street vendors who call out little tunes, *pregónes*, about what they are selling. The practice goes back to the days of the colonial era and the market vendors who sang testaments to their vegetables and other wares. Socialism in its most dour, anti-market phase in the 1960s and 1970s all but wiped out small business, and thus *pregoneros* too. But they are returning with a vengeance. Art festivals, such as the Havana Biennial, have recently included exhibitions and live performances of *pregoneros*, now heralded as practitioners of a lost art form.

A number of popular Cuban songs of the 1920s and 1930s started as *pregónes*, the most famous being Moisés Simons' "*El Manisero*" (The Peanut Vendor). It was recorded by Rita Montaner in 1928, but many will also remember Cary Grant letting loose and singing it in the 1939 film *Only Angels Have Wings*.

> If you haven't got bananas don't be blue
> Peanuts in a little bag are calling you
> Don't waste them {no tummy ache}

You'll taste them {when you're awake}
For at the very break of day
The peanut vendor's on his way
At dawning the whistle blows
{through every city, town and country lane
you hear him sing his plaintive little strain}
And as he goes by to you he'll say
Mani! (Peanuts)[8]

The last word is drawn out, as in Maaaannniiiiii.

Another *pregón*-inspired song was released in 1994, recorded by the duo Gema and Pavel. Their song, *"Helado Sobre Ruedas"* (Ice Cream on Wheels), is a sad tribute to the melodies of the ice-cream cart, which had disappeared from Havana's streets during the Special Period. Canadian sound researcher Vincent Adrisani writes elegantly about how the sound of the ice cream vendor "echoes the complex history of the city."[9]

In 2012, Maria Magdalena Campos-Pons and Neil Leonard organized *pregonero* exhibitions and competitions at the Havana Biennial. They say the return of the *pregoneros* is changing the soundscape of Cuba, turning the streets into musical theatre. What they call an "ancient vocal marketing strategy" takes up where the lack of large-scale private business culture leaves off.[10] Cuba's billboards sell ideology and history, not toothpaste. Cuban products such as coffee or rum are advertised in print media and posters, but there are as yet no product advertisements on Cuban TV.[11] This startling reality was something I only fully appreciated in Canada, watching an episode of *The Office* with Zaira, a Cuban student, during her first weeks in Canada when she was living in our house.

48 ★

A pregoneru
competition,
Prado,
Old Havana,
June 2015

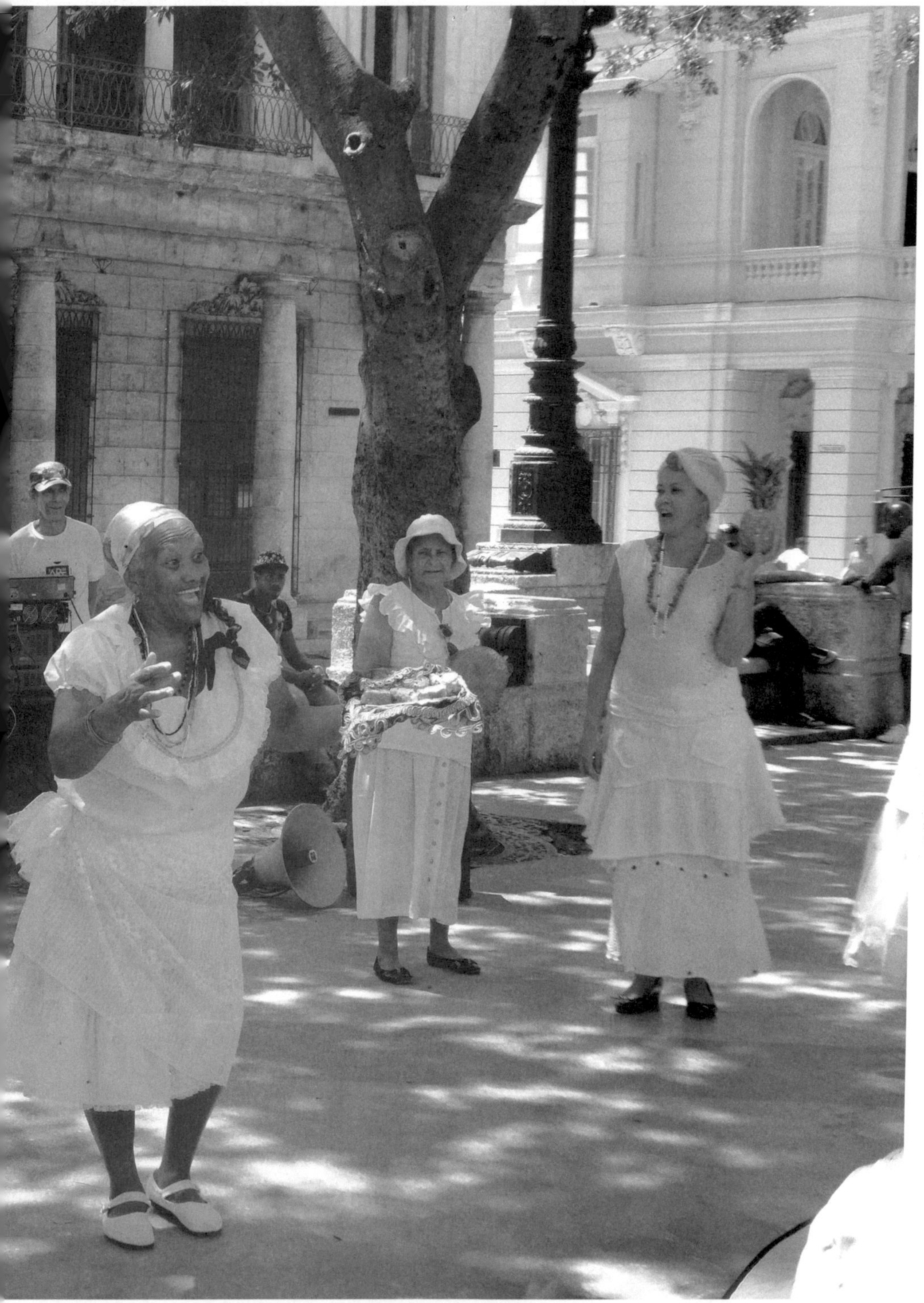

When the first commercial came on, she shrieked in delight. "Oh my god, is this one of those *commercials?*" she asked, delighted, at age twenty-eight, to see her first TV ad.

So *pregoneros* have the advertising field to themselves. The *maniseros* of Old Havana are legendary. I've seen one woman in particular, who sometimes dresses in colonial-era garb, interviewed on Cuban TV. Her name is Elena and she's easy to spot on the crooked narrow streets of Old Havana. She occasionally sings *"El Manisero"* in a deep, beautiful voice.

Recently I came across a *pregonera* competition, of sorts: a group of women, each singing tribute to the product—pineapples, cupcakes, flowers—they were selling. It took place on the busy pedestrian mall in the centre of Prado in Old Havana, and the women attracted an appreciative crowd. But it's not just the peanut vendors in the tourist-laden squares and plazas of Old Havana who sing. The residential streets of Havana are filled with people wheeling carts of flowers or vegetables, or carrying towels, brooms, or beautiful strands of onion or garlic braided together. Their melodious voices can make the most mundane household items sound divine. Take "chlorine," for example. In Spanish, *cloro* trills off the end of a *pregón* like a bird. There are also *pregoneros* who roam the streets promising to buy gold, "whatever little piece of gold," they repeatedly chant. A musical duo incorporated this *pregón* into a popular song, parodying youth culture's obsession with gold jewelry. Life-long Havana residents Olguita and Inés told me about their favourite neighbourhood *pregonero*, who calls out seeking "empty perfume bottles, brand name," which he fills with something aromatic and then resells. The neighbourhood *pregoneros* are not all as impressive as Elena, the famous *manisera* of Old Havana, but they add a melodic feature to the noisy soundscape of the city. And it's a great sales technique. When I first heard the onion vendor, I didn't realize he was selling entire strands—about ten onions—as one unit. I tried to explain that I was in Havana alone for a couple of weeks and just needed a few onions. He smiled. "Don't you have any friends you could share it with?" he asked me.

CERRO AND MY GAY TRADE UNION

Peeking out just to the left of the hard-to-miss Plaza de la Revolucion is the Estadio Latinoamericano, the baseball stadium located in a neighbourhood called Cerro. Attending a baseball game would be the only reason for most foreign visitors to go to Cerro. Baseball games are fun in Havana, but it is the visitor's loss if that's their only destination. Cerro is a conglomeration of unpainted, twisting, narrow streets, much less classically scenic than Old Havana, and with a much denser population than Vedado, its two closest neighbours. It isn't central, but neither is it difficult to get to. Like plenty of poor neighbourhoods—in Havana I always want to say "more poor"—it shows its sense of pride and despair in equal measure. An artist friend who lives there tells me a story which she says is pure Cerro. There was a large meat-processing plant there for many years, but during the Special Period the government closed it. The reason was not, ultimately, because of the endemic livestock or fuel shortages, but because the workers, knowing their neighbours were hungry, were constantly throwing cuts of meat out the window at people waiting below.

Cerro isn't as dense as Centro Habana, another poor neighbourhood that bisects Vedado and Old Havana, because its buildings are lower rise, and generally in better shape—which isn't saying much. More than any neighbourhood I have seen, it is a place where people live life on the streets. Men bring out card tables and chairs to play dominoes. During the baseball playoffs, if the beloved Havana team, the Industriales, are playing, people string cords for the TV and put it outside to watch together, along with most of their living room furniture. Often I make the hour-long trek from Vedado to Cerro by foot up calle G, toward Revolution Square, passing behind the National Library toward the baseball stadium. Once you get into "deep Cerro," the street life is continuous, in all seasons and at all times of day. It is a neighbourhood unfrequented by tourists, so I pass unnoticed.

My usual destination in Cerro is Mirta's house. There are several things to look forward to when I know I can spend a Sunday afternoon there. One is the house itself. She lives in an apartment complex known as "los edificios de Pastorita"—Pastorita's buildings. Pastorita was Pastorita Nuñez, a rare gem of a bureaucrat who, right after the revolution, oversaw the construction of several apartment complexes that remain great testaments to utopian dreams of social housing that actually worked. They are exactly the opposite of the Soviet-inspired nightmares outside Havana in Alamar—buildings that appeared in the decidedly less utopian era of 1970s. Pastorita's buildings are utilitarian, but they don't look like the crumbling cages that house poor people in Alamar, New York, Toronto, and everywhere else in the world. Mirta's apartment complex is low-rise, relatively low-density, and looks out onto a lush banana grove. The buildings were designed for maximum airflow, and the balconies provide both privacy and shade.

The second reason to be happy to receive an invitation to Mirta's is the food; this is closely related to the third and best reason: Mirta and her friends. They are excellent cooks. When I am in town, Mirta and her friends always summon me to what they call a meeting of our *sindicato*, our union: Mirta's house is the centre of gay Cerro.

Mirta, Lina, Jorge, and Omar make up the nucleus of the group, though on any given visit plenty of other people, gay and straight, young and old, pass through. This particular gay union local would probably not be recognized as such if one were expecting gay by current North American standards. Gay Cerro ranges in age from Jorge, a youthful forty-five, to seventy-two-year-old Lina. No one is sleek or fashionably dressed. Everyone is poor, even by Cuban standards. Mirta and Lina live on tiny retirement incomes, Jorge is a nurse, and Omar cleans houses and collects groceries for his neighbours. Mirta is the rare habanero I know who lives alone, though recently she's started to take in tenants from a nearby campus of the international medical school. Her latest student tenant is Emilio, from San Francisco. Emilio grew up the son of a Mexican immigrant farm worker and cannot believe that he has the good fortune to find himself among the 15,000 foreign students training for free in Cuba to become doctors. Mirta can't believe the irony of having found a tenant from San Francisco, the gayest town in the world, who is avidly heterosexual. They make an adorable couple.

Mirta inherited the apartment as payment from an old woman she looked after for decades. Job options for unmarried women of Mirta's generation were slim. A surprising number of gay and lesbian habaneros I know have similar career paths, working in the social service or medical field, as nurses or caregivers of various sorts, though I've also met several lesbian doctors. It's tempting to try to generalize this, at least for the men, as part of the overall stereotype that gay equals feminine equals caregiving, and maybe there's something to that. Despite much publicized recent advances in transgender rights and lesbian and gay rights under the leadership of the (straight) Mariela Castro, Raúl's high-profile daughter, being gay in Cuba is still not what one might call a wise career move.

Or at least it wasn't when my friends from Cerro came of age a generation or two ago. Susan Belyea and I once attended Havana's Pride Day with our Cerro trade union. It was a relatively small but boisterous event, which paraded down La Rampa on 23 Street, about as central as it's possible to be. It ended with the inevitable, a speech by Mariela Castro. We were certainly among the oldest people in the group, but that probably would have been true in any group of gay people celebrating Pride Day anywhere. This generation of gay Cubans tends not to attend other non-state sanctioned events like the "kiss-in" that gay rights groups have started holding in some of the prominent plazas of Old Havana. They don't frequent Havana's handful of gay bars either. I met Mirta through Isabel, her former partner, who works in the art world. Isabel told me that in their early years together, she would occaslonally introduce Mirta as her aunt (Mirta is a decade older) at work functions or other social events. And this is in the art world. Of course, gay people, in Cuba as in any other part of the world, who came out in an earlier, less forgiving era, often hold on to residual suspicions, for good reason. In Havana I can never tell if this level of caution is overblown or not. In all my time there I've never experienced overt or even subtle homophobia, but as a foreigner—and a middle-aged mother—I am also quite protected.

In deep Cerro, being gay seems less of an issue than being poor. Some of my gay friends' distance from what is becoming an organized and visible gay community in Havana has to do with money: They don't have disposable income to spend in bars or on evening wear. Another Cerro friend was recently told by ETECSA—the much-hated, state-owned Cuban telephone company—that her request for a landline in her apartment was at the bottom of the priority list because they have no plans to expand or improve services in Cerro. None. Not "next month" or "next year". Rather, she was assured she would *never* have a landline in Cerro. It reminded me of a story from a Canadian friend, who once heard World Bank representatives explain to an international NGO gathering that Africa wasn't on its global financial projections because "it just didn't figure."

Cerro just doesn't figure in La Nueva Cuba, where the trend toward free market economic reforms has more to do with the freshly painted buildings of Old Havana and the shockingly good new restaurants in Vedado—which is why these days the long walk to Mirta's house in Cerro gives me an even greater perspective on why I'm proud to be a member of this particular union. It's the only Cuban house I've been in where the men also cook. Jorge and Omar also clean up, and Mirta bosses them around and tells them what they've overlooked. The TV is always on, blaring telenovelas, or a strange assortment of US programs, or sports. During a memorable World Cup Sunday, Jorge openly ogled the players' bums and Omar pretended he didn't know what sport was being broadcast. "What, baseball season again?" he kept saying. The telephone rang constantly, Emilio blared Mexican hip hop from his room, and heavenly smells wafted from the kitchen.

During another visit we all got to talking about wine. Cerro's rare, and unlikely, entry into the entrepreneurial world of La Nueva Cuba is a new winery, La Canal, which sells wine made from a range of unusual plants. Mirta had bought a bottle of watercress wine for us to sample. It was tasty, yet Lina pronounced her preference for French. Someone asked her, teasingly, if she had ever been to France (knowing full well she had never left Cuba in her life). "No," she said, "but I hope to go sometime." This declaration from a seventy-something, retired, poor Third World lesbian sipping watercress wine could have been pitiable or ridiculous. But, in true Cerro style, it was stated firmly and optimistically. When, on my next visit, I arrived with a small bottle of good French wine for Lina, she accepted my gift graciously. But she was a step ahead of me. She told me she was leaving Cuba for a six-month visit to the US. An ex-girlfriend had invited her, sent her a plane ticket, and the US granted her a visitor's visa. Miami isn't Paris. But she plans to sample all the wine she can get her hands on.

WOMEN, MEN, AND THE EVERYDAY BATTLES OF THE STREET

If I had to select one difference between Cubans and North Americans it would have to be how strangers interact with each other. Better said, in Cuba strangers *do* interact with each other. This can be both a blessing and a curse. The best known and most obvious example is the active interest taken by Cuban men in women—*any* woman, almost. My Spanish teacher Carolina, a smart, accomplished woman in her sixties, told me that when men stopped commenting on her appearance on the street, she realized she was old. When I heard that, I immediately put her into the category I, like many North American feminists, carry with me almost unconsciously: smart women who need to up their feminist game. Some years later I have a different, more complicated view of what she told me, and not just because I can now see the advance of sixty myself.

The female students I bring to Havana from Canada walk the streets in shock for the first few days, aghast at the amount of attention they receive from men. We prepare them by trying to explain that there are different sexual cultures in the world. We try to get them to understand that Cuban women themselves distinguish between *piropos*—flattering compliments about appearance—and *groseros*—lewd or aggressive remarks. I've heard it said that Cuban women in Canada start to wonder how they look, because so few people comment on their appearance. However, the distinction between flattering and insulting commentary by men is lost on twenty-year-old Canadians, and not only because most of them don't understand the rapid-fire Spanish that they hear on Havana streets. What is easy to miss, for the foreigner, is that street interactions between women and men in Cuba are often also about men proving themselves among other men. Who can come up with the most daring, lewd *grosero* or, alternatively, who can express the most creative, seductive *piropo?*[12] For those of us from cultures where people barely make eye contact on the street, these distinctions barely matter.

At the extreme end of the *groseros* are the public masturbators, a form of street interaction in which the patriarchal underpinnings of all of this become—pardon the pun—unzipped and obvious. There's a relatively deserted stretch of calle G (on the maps it's Avenida de los Presidentes, a name no one uses) that leads to the Faculty of Arts and Letters at the University of Havana, where my students take classes. The combination of a deserted stretch of street, enormous trees to provide cover, and a steady stream of young women walking to school makes this area a magnet for Havana's public masturbators. Of course this isn't only a Cuban issue. The seawall of Stanley Park in Vancouver, for example, provides exactly the same cover. But the many Cuban feminists—female and male—who have agitated about this issue are frustrated that it is sometimes tolerated as "just how Cuban men are." A valiant University of Havana expert on masculinity, Julio César González Pagés, regularly regales our students with stories of Havana's public masturbators, some funny, some horrific. But he also talks about the work that he, his students, and many others are doing to try to transform this practice of male sexuality as spectator sport.

During one recent visit my students had an especially hard time coping with all of this. It doesn't take fluent Spanish to understand the difference between an admiring *"que linda"* (how beautiful) and a snarling *"que puta"* (what a slut), which they were hearing repeatedly. So a bunch of them decided to escape into pure, anonymous tourism, and went off to the beach in Varadero during their free Sunday. I understood, but was disappointed that they were missing a tranquil Havana Sunday. Even more so when I realized it was Mother's Day. I experienced a whole other side of patriarchal Havana street culture that day, because on Mother's Day men in Havana greet women who look like they might be mothers (that is, just about any adult woman) with a smiling, respectful *"felicidades"* (congratulations). The same thing happens on March 8, International Women's Day. In North America, the occasion barely registers, except among feminist activists. In Cuba it's another opportunity to greet women on the street but, in my experience at least, with no underlying hostility. One year when I happened to be there on March 8, my landlord made a point of coming by to give me a rose.

Cuban street culture is as different from my own as it is possible to be. The other figure that attracts a huge amount of attention from strangers on the street is the baby or young child. When my son was young he would be touched, cuddled, even picked up by strangers, usually women, cooing *"que lindo."* Among adults as well, Cubans can be extraordinarily affectionate. Plenty of tourists have complaints about the on-again, off-again service culture in hotels and restaurants. I too have seen plenty of rude, unfriendly store clerks or waiters. But I've also seen, particularly in places less frequented by visitors, such as vegetable markets, how commercial transactions are regularly punctuated with endearments: *mi vida, mi amor, mi cielo, mi corazon, querida, papi, mami* — my life, my love, my heaven, my heart, my dear. You can get a great deal of affection just in buying tomatoes. On the other hand, sometimes strangers scold, like the time a vegetable vendor freaked out at the sight of my four-year-old boy with nail polish on, telling him (and me) sternly, "In Cuba, boys don't do that." I've had museum guards take my son off my hands so I could concentrate on touring the museum, and women in restaurants invite him to sit with them and finish their pizza. Such things are supposed to panic me, and him, in Canada, but in Cuba "don't talk to strangers" just doesn't register.

But to me the best example of how Cuban personal interactions are different from those of most Canadians is the way they line up. And they do, a lot. Approaching a bus stop or a pizza kiosk, the untrained eye might see just a random group of people milling about. That's the *ultimo* system. Each person approaches the group and asks for *el ultimo:* who is the last one here? The last person acknowledges him or herself. And so the new person remains *el ultimo* until the next person comes along and takes on the responsibility themselves. Once you are thus inserted into the lineup you are free to wander a bit, find a patch of shade perhaps, secure in the knowledge that your place in the order of things is safe. It's a good metaphor for the country as a whole actually. It looks like a disorganized, random mess, but it functions because people still talk to each other.

THE FUTUROS COMMUNISTAS DAYCARE CENTRE AND OTHER ANOMALIES OF CUBAN CHILDHOOD

My first extended time in Havana was in 2004, when I spent almost six months there researching the curious tale of Operation Peter Pan. This was something that began right after the Revolution, in 1960, and involved over 14,000 Cuban children leaving Havana for Miami. They travelled alone, unaccompanied by their parents. In Miami, those who did not have family awaiting them went into the care of the Catholic Welfare Bureau, whose director had been given the unprecedented power by the US government to waive visa requirements for arriving Cuban children.

This mass migration took place because of the fears of jittery middle-class Cuban parents about what might become of their children when Fidel Castro came to power. The months after the revolution were certainly tumultuous; but such fears were, at least in part, flamed by an assortment of CIA-sponsored rumours. US-funded radio stations and printing presses worked overtime, circulating stories that Castro was about to nationalize children and send them to the Soviet Union for indoctrination. Another variant was that the new daycares springing up in the early years of the revolution were going to be used as permanent dormitories in which to lodge children. When Cuban-American relations ruptured completely after the Bay of Pigs invasion of 1961, thousands of Cuban children were essentially stuck in the US, separated from their parents for many years, some permanently. In a story full of tragic ironies, one remains glaring: parental custody rights were indeed abrogated, but not by the Cubans. As US academic Ramón de la Campa, a former Peter Pan child, has put it, "We ended up in camps after all. We were saved from Prague but were sent instead to naval bases in Opa-Locka, orphanages in Toledo, camps in Jacksonville."[13]

I learned about Operation Peter Pan through the story of another famous globetrotting Cuban child, when I joined much of North America following the saga of Elián González in 1999. He was the six-year-old child who left Cuba on a rickety boat with his mother, her boyfriend, and several others to make the short but dangerous journey to Miami. The boat capsized and only Elián survived. He was taken in by his uncle and other family members in Miami, despite the request of his father in Cuba that he be returned. The ensuing standoff between both branches of the González family became just one more high-profile American TV saga of the pre-social media era. US media avidly followed Elián's Miami family as they immersed him in American childhood, as though each toy truck and trip to Disneyworld would cleanse or rebirth him. For their part, Cubans, viewing the story as a kidnapping, organized huge mass rallies in Havana demanding his return. A typical image that circulated in Cuban media in that era was Mickey Mouse ears hitched to a ball and chain. Finally the two governments brokered a deal which saw the child taken at gunpoint from his recalcitrant Miami relatives (who had exhausted their legal appeals to keep the boy against the wishes of his father) and returned to Cuba.

It was a dramatic, captivating story. It was yet another example of Cuba's position as ground zero in an ongoing Cold War, but it also showed how even small children can figure centrally in international political conflicts. Because of the intense family pain that this story exposed, I had ambivalent feelings about gawking, even through the remoteness of my TV screen. But my interest was piqued because I was already thinking about children crossing borders and what this tells us about global inequalities and conflicts. Elián's story mirrored, almost exactly, the timeline of the adoption of my son from Guatemala. He was born in November 1999, the same month that Elián was found clinging to an inner tube off the coast of Miami. Elián left for Cuba with his father in June 2000, just a couple of weeks after we returned from Guatemala to Canada with six-month-old Jordi.

In 2004 I lived with my family, Susan Belyea and Jordi, in Havana for six months to research Operation Peter Pan. It seemed a perfect example to add to my study of how child migration stories can produce powerful national and international political tensions. There were many reasons Elián struck such a chord among Cubans—wherever they lived—but surely one of them was that a generation earlier over 14,000 young Cubans had some of the same painful experiences. With that history, it is easy to see why Cuba is a gold mine for people who study children and international politics. When I got there in 2004, Elián himself had faded from the news in both countries, though he re-emerges occasionally in Cuba. Throughout his childhood he popped up in the Cuban media, accompanying Fidel Castro at various events such as International Children's Day. He also circulates in Cuba's underground world of humour. Like this joke I first heard in 2004:

> It's the year 2020 and a man is running along the Malecón yelling, "Return Elián! Return Elián!" "Comrade," says another man to him, "the Americans returned Elián to Cuba years ago." "I know," says the yelling man, "I'm Elián."

Living with a Guatemalan-born child when I was researching childhood in Havana, with the popular memory of both Elián and his Peter Pan predecessors still very much alive—all this gave me a great deal to think about. And it was more than an academic exercise; I had skin in the game. So what was it like for a four-year-old English-speaking Guatemalan-Canadian to spend his tender years in Havana? We quickly realized that fighting the formidable Cuban bureaucracy to try to enroll him in daycare was not likely to be an easy battle, and the option of enrolling him in the English-language school for diplomats' children defeated one of our reasons for being there: to speak Spanish. Instead, Vanessa, the female half of the couple from whom we rented our apartment, did double duty as part-time childminder. At the end of our first six-month stint in Havana, Jordi had developed an impressive Spanish vocabulary, an awesome Cuban accent, and a heavy sugar dependency. "Do all Canadians think sugar is bad for children or just you two?" Vanessa asked us one day. We all developed a fondness for Cuban TV cartoons, which replay endlessly around five o'clock, at the end of the long workday. To this day, singer Liuba María Hevia's beautiful video cartoon about Estela, the dreadlock-wearing *granito de canela* (little speck of cinnamon) who didn't want to fall into the pot, makes me tear up, perhaps because I saw it daily for months on end. I think of this tiny bit of cross-cultural infantile nostalgia as my version of what Cubans of my generation have plenty of: a huge fondness for the Soviet-era cartoons they grew up with on Cuban TV.

So, I don't have direct institutional knowledge about how Havana daycares or schools care for children, but I learned plenty about the rest of the village. I've already described the easy intimacy with children on the part of Cuban people, and this affection includes foreign children. A visiting Canadian friend began joking that Cubans must think his infant son was named "Lindo" because everywhere they went he heard murmurs of "*que lindo*" (how cute). Of course, plenty of other cultures express the same easy conviviality toward other people's children, a trait notably lacking in much of North America. This isn't especially Cuban, though a Havana friend once explained the obviously child-worshipping ways of his culture in pointedly political terms. The deprivations of the Special Period still resonate, and those who grew up or parented in the early 1990s now lavish as much as they can on children, as though to exorcise the memories of sending children to school (or being sent themselves) after a breakfast of nothing more than sugar water and fried mango skin.

Growing up part-time in Havana gave my son many things, including a healthy attitude about people he doesn't know: he neither fears nor is suspicious of strangers. The most telling lesson I think I learned while raising a child in Havana occurred every time we passed one of our local Vedado daycare centres, the name of which was announced on a brightly painted sign: Futuros Communistas. There are a wide variety of perspectives about childhood in the world, and especially their relationship to politics.

A national system of childcare was one of several sweeping social welfare reforms ushered in by the revolutionary government in 1959. The first Circulos Infantiles (Infant Circles or daycare centres), thirty-seven in total, were opened in 1961, and expanded rapidly thereafter. By the mid-1960s, Cuba was spending more on childcare per capita than any country in the world.[14] In 1970 there were over 600 centres. They were created, administered, and staffed by the newly formed Cuban Federation of Women (FMC), a new national organization, itself a product of the revolution. Like all achievements in health and social welfare, the *circulos* suffered during the Special Period. However, none closed. Indeed, the country had expanded the number of childcare centres by the end of the 1990s, and today they number approximately 1,156.[15] Strong government support for the *circulos* in the 1960s

CIRCULO INFANTIL
Futuros comunistas

CIRCULO INFANTIL
Los compañeritos

★ 67

Circulo Infantil Futuros Communistas
Circulo Infantil Los Compañeritos (Little Comrades)
Circulo Infantil Vanuardia de América (Vanguard of America)
Circulo Infantil *Blanca Nieves* (Snow White)

reflected the convergence of two trends: increased demand for female participation in the labour force and the elevation of children and youth as political, indeed revolutionary, subjects. To see the latter claim, you just have to read the signs.

The array of names and images that grace the *circulos* is an integral part of Havana's streetscapes. In a city that is famous for looking so different from other parts of the world—old cars, old buildings, no recognizable North American brand signs—the *circulos*, though more discreet than revolutionary billboards, contribute to this kaleidoscope of visual difference. Turn a corner and you receive an instant lesson in history and politics. Daycares are named after an array of Cuban and global revolutionary figures (Celia Sánchez, Camilo Cienfuegos, Che Guevera, Rosa Luxemburg, Simón Bolivar, and José Martí, to name a few); they offer faint reminders of bygone solidarities ("Heroic Vietnam," "Little Friends of Poland," "Beautiful Chile"), as well as what were once the hopeful dreams for the future ("The Little Comrades," "The Little Proletariat," "The Vanguard of America," "Future Combatants"). Occasionally, they represent a version of childhood that might be cloyingly recognizable to North Americans ("Snow White," "Little Champions," "Happy Little Cubans"). But more often, signs such as "Proletarian Gentlemen," "Little Internationalists," and, of course, "Future Communists" offer a very different way of thinking about childhood.

In the 1960s, the revolutionary names selected for childcare centres were not just leftist whimsy; they were an indication of something profound. The social reforms in the Cuba of the early 1960s were nothing if not ambitious and utopian, and this held for children as much as anyone else, perhaps more so. From the newly designed collective playpens, to the celebration of group birthdays, to a completely innovative curriculum, the *circulos* in the 1960s were the first steps in the new society and new personality that the Cuban Revolution sought to create, from the bottom up. The *circulos* were just one part of a vast new education system that was going to change everything. The children of "The Little Proletariat" daycare centre might continue on to primary and secondary schools with a curriculum that was both rigorous and didactic. In high school they might have spent time in residential country schools where they cut sugar cane or sewed gym clothes part-time for their keep. If they were really smart (and/or politically connected) they might have attended the Centro Vocacional de Lenin, "La Lenin," as it's known, the most elite and desirable of Havana's residential high schools. I have heard adult Cubans toss around their "La Lenin" credentials in exactly the same snobby manner as Americans drop their Harvard or Yale creds—oblivious, seemingly, to the biting irony—to my North American ear—of trying to cash in on that particular name. All of this education, including university, remains free.

Today, this vision of sentimentalized children and revolutionary nostalgia is repeated constantly outside the daycare centres of every neighbourhood in the city. I think the names both prove and disprove "The Dreams of Che" (*Los Sueños del Che*), and indeed all of the dreams of the 1960s. One day when I was visiting Mirta in Cerro I started musing about the weirdness of the Future Communist daycare I passed daily in Vedado. Were all the daycares in Havana named like this, I asked her? Does it seem weird to you that daycares have names like "Little Proletariat?"

Mirta walked over to a drawer, retrieved her Havana telephone book, thumbed through it, and wordlessly ripped out a few pages. She handed me the names and addresses of the hundreds of Havana *circulos* and said, "Go find out." So, shortly after I asked one of my few friends with a car in Havana to drive me around the city and the suburbs in order to take photos of daycare centres and their intriguing signs. Aldo humoured me, as he always does, and we spent a day driving around and taking photos. If daycare employees looked at me and my camera disapprovingly, he would reassure them, "Don't worry, she's from Pastors for Peace," a trusted US NGO that brings medical and educational supplies to Cuba. Another time he announced I was from the *New York Times*. But when Aldo caught sight of the wretched condition of the building that housed "The Constructors of the Future" daycare, he'd had enough infantile optimism. "If these are the Constructors of the Future," he muttered to me, "we're fucked."

Cuban daycare centres have suffered as the Cuban government retrenches its social service spending. Like many state-owned facilities in poor repair, plenty stay closed for years waiting for repairs. In 2015, the state press reported enthusiastically that eleven had been reopened in Havana after closures that had lasted up to seven years.[16] Yet over fifty centres remain closed, awaiting repairs or personnel in various municipalities throughout the country.[17] Childcare workers in Cuba, like childcare workers the world over, are among the lowest-paid workers in their country ($340 MN, $13 CUC); they are at the bottom of the Cuban pay scale.[18] While the vast majority of authorized *cuentapropismo* (self-employment) is in the restaurants and service industries, private daycares are becoming increasingly common.

Now middle-class parents have the option of paying monthly fees that range from $40–$120 CUC for private daycare, instead of the equivalent of less than $2 monthly in the state-run *circulos*. Not surprisingly, private centres offer better food, supplies, and child/teacher ratios. But with all things Cuban, a little perspective goes a long way. Recent research tells us that UNICEF's minimum standards for childcare are met by only *one* First World country.[19] That this iconography—as retro as it is—graces a functioning (barely, but functioning) national system of subsidized childcare in a poor Third World country is perhaps the greatest anomaly of all.

TWO

THOSE WHO DREAM WITH THEIR EARS: THE SOUND OF HAVANA

WALKING OUT INTO THE NIGHT MUSIC: RANDOM HORNS AND EVERYDAY REGGAETÓN

One of my first experiences of the sound of Havana occurred in a moment, as I was walking one evening in Vedado near the beautiful old theatre, Amadeo Roldán. A young man stepped out of his house just as I was passing. He put a trumpet to his lips and began playing, simply and beautifully, as I walked past. It was night, not very late, and the music followed me as I continued walking down calle Calzada toward my apartment.

A random, lone trumpet sounding melodically in the city night sky, it's almost a clichéd Hollywood image, but it happens from time to time in Havana. If you can't wait for a random moment, take a walk along avenida Boyeros, near the Omnibus Terminal, not far from Revolution Square. Across the street is a stadium where, owing to the great acoustics provided by the cement awnings, horn players regularly gather to practice. The same thing happens on the Malecón, near the statue of Antonio Maceo, where an underpass (which is always closed) also attracts horn players. Geographers claim that music is how Havana neighbourhoods are transformed from "space to place"—traditional *son* is the sound of tourist-heavy Old Havana, drums are persistent in predominantly Afro Cuban Centro, and internationally inflected jazz reigns in cosmopolitan Vedado.[1] Personally, I hear more of a mixture than a boundary when I walk these streets, but the point is, Havana is a musical city.

The richness of Cuban music has drawn attention and visitors for over a century. "Why is Cuban music so good?" is a question I pose as research to my Canadian students, fully and ironically aware that this formulation skews the results. But that is my point: we can begin the discussion from the premise that Cuban music is "so good." There are plenty of ways to explore why that is so, but most would agree that syncretism or cultural mixing provides part of the answer. Cuban music mixes historical and geographic influences like nothing else. In Havana one can appreciate not only the immense quality of Cuban music but also its variety. Genres such as salsa, son, bolero, mambo, and jazz are familiar to foreign audiences because of how they have crossed borders. In Havana one can hear the full range of traditional or classical Cuban sounds, as well as genres that might take visitors by surprise: *trova* (which is comparable to folk), hip hop, rock, reggaetón, metal, and country have all been remixed and reinterpreted in distinctly Cuban ways.

There are dozens of venues in Havana to hear some of the best music of the world. I can still hear Kervin Barreto playing the classic *"Viente Años"* (Twenty Years) on his trumpet at the

La Zorra y el Cuervo, a popular jazz club on La Rampa in Vedado. I have been deliriously happy hearing a range of different music from the undulating 1950s balconies at the Mella Theatre on calle Línea, under the stars at the beautiful outdoor club el Sauce in Playa, as well as at two other popular venues, el Brecht and the Fábrica de Arte Cubano. However, walking the street, day or night, is almost like attending an ambulatory concert—or rather a series of concerts. In Havana "garage bands" are rooftop bands or balcony bands or courtyard bands, audible at various levels all over the neighbourhood. If you live near a park or community centre you don't need to know the schedule of musical events during the weekend, because a strong breeze and an open window (which all of them mostly are) will deliver the sound right to your apartment. One December evening during the Havana Jazz Festival I decided, after a lot of late nights in a row, I needed a night in. Reluctantly, I stayed home to catch up on some sleep. I should have known better. That night, right from my bed, I listened to one of my favourite ensemble groups, Interactivo, perform outdoors at a cultural centre two blocks from my apartment—the same beautiful set that had done me in when I had heard them play the night before in a club.

All this music-making doesn't just happen. It is a cliché that Cuban musicians are among the best in the world, but it's not by magic.[3] The Cuban revolution built a tremendous education system in the early years, and music education was no exception. Here they built on a pre-existing tradition of musicianship, handed down from generation to generation. Cuba's long history as a tourist destination actually nurtured this musicianship, as generations of fathers taught generations of sons (and occasionally daughters) to perform old standbys like *"Guantanamera"* for generations of tourists. After 1959, the Cuban government expanded and formalized this training, turning golf courses into music schools and opening countless neighbourhood *casas de cultura*, cultural centres. The new government closed the nightclubs and casinos, and plenty of world-famous musicians such as Celia Cruz left for Miami and New York. But those who stayed saw a different kind of musical culture develop, which emphasizes performance over album sales, and provides sophisticated education even when the most basic elements like proper instruments remain scarce. Even through the Soviet years of grey, ideological rigidity, music remained defiantly Cuban, and both musicians and audiences alike are educated and selective.[3] Cuba is one of the few places in the world where, when a child declares their intention to be a musician, parents might actually be pleased.

The emphasis on performance over recording doesn't make musicians wealthy, but it expands their skill and their repertoire. It also provides them with a bit of ammunition against censorship. Censorship hides in plain sight in Cuba. I know a couple of young, hip art students who work part-time for the Cuban TV station as censors. It is their job to scan foreign TV shows before they are broadcast and bleep political references that the Cuban government doesn't like. They are given a list of key symbols or words to look for—US flags or critical references to Cuba or communism, for example—then they just edit them out. They are as committed to this as my own students in Canada are to serving coffee or slinging beer; it's a job, nothing more.

For musicians, censorship is a bit more complex because performing live always allows for a dynamic relationship between artist and audience. The state retaliates by controlling access to the airwaves and concert venues, but, despite that, popular Cuban musicians maintain strong and organic bonds with their audiences. Musician Carlos Varela made gentle fun of his experiences with censorship in song, laconically summing up their efforts in "*Memorias*":

> "Sometimes they play me on the radio,
> Sometimes they don't." [4]

Cubans can take matters—and voices—into their own hands to thwart the censors. Concerts are a delight to be part of in Havana because everyone sings. Joaquín Borges-Triana, one of Cuba's premier music writers, told me once that in Cuba it's like the musicians are accompanying the audience rather than the other way around. It seems that everyone knows the lyrics to everything. Concerts are more like conversations, or perhaps choral festivals. But even non-concert venues can give people cause to sing. I once attended a screening of a Spanish-made documentary about Silvio Rodríguez, one of the founding fathers of contemporary Cuban music, revered by several generations since he emerged in the 1960s. One of his signature songs played through the credits, and even as the lights came up I watched hundreds of movie-goers remain in their seats singing happily along with Silvio on the screen.

These days, to the frustration of many, the real music of the people is reggaetón, which is not known for its complexity, musicianship, or lyrics. The driving beats of reggaetón (the "ón" adds force; it could be translated as "reggae max" or "big reggae") are a mix of electronics and vocals. It's a mix of Jamaican, Puerto Rican, and Trinidadian sounds, though as it circulates every nation puts their on imprint on it. It is now the ambient sound of just about every Havana neighbourhood, apartment building, store, and taxi (at least the inexpensive ones). Taking a bus to the large concert venues such as Teatro Karlos Marx in Miramar—a mammoth 5,000-seat theatre—can be just as much of a musical event as the concert itself. On the night buses, reggaetón blasts from headphones, cellphones, and portable devices of various kinds. People move as though on a dance floor. My Canadian friend Ruth tells me she saw someone hang a disco ball in a crowded bus as it sped along.

Despite the sometimes-intense sexism of the lyrics (almost inaudible to me, however, in its rapid-fire, slangy street Spanish), I'm not so bothered by reggaetón, even when it's blasting from the neighbour's balcony below me, or from a taxi I'm in. Musicians hate reggaetón because of its low level of musicianship, but others complain more about its explicit hypersexuality. Joaquín Borges-Triana questions this moralistic condemnation of reggaetón, noting that such criticisms "reflect a longstanding tradition of denying sexuality and pleasure to women."[5] Geoffrey Baker, an English musicologist, tells a great story about how a visiting Harry Belafonte took Fidel Castro aside in 1999 to convince him that hip hop, as a genre, should not be simply dismissed as *"la música del enemigo"*—the music of the enemy, as US popular music such as rock had been branded since the 1960s in Cuba.[6] For Belafonte, hip hop—like rock and roll before it—was a global, powerful art form, from which Cuban youth should not be excluded. He seems to have had some success convincing

Castro of his position. Every generation demonizes a type of music, and blames it for all kinds of social problems.

Of course there are fans of particular musical genres in Cuba. But the general Cuban enthusiasm for music of all styles, genres, and varieties is palpable. "Market segments" among the audience are almost unknown or indistinguishable from each other. I am always shocked by the level of musical awareness, knowledge, and appreciation I see in Havana. I have conversations about the latest hip hop group with colleagues in their seventies. One afternoon in a Havana pool I watched a sixty-something Cuban woman dancing, beer in one hand, grandchild's hand in another, to the tune of the popular reggaetón hit "*Loco sexual.*" A concert of almost any sort draws a vast demographic, and the repertoire of the black-clad kids in their twenties who congregate in the evenings on calle G occasionally includes Silvio Rodríguez classics from the 1960s. The whole country is a playlist.

HOW CUBAN MUSIC MADE ME A BETTER HISTORIAN

"If you want to learn anything about the history of this country, you have to start listening to Carlos Varela." This advice, offered by Caridad Cumaná, a Cuban colleague who was helping me make my way through a Havana film archive, proved remarkably true. When I came to Cuba to research political conflicts about child migration in 2004, I also gained a huge appreciation for music as a form of truth-telling and social commentary. Carlos Varela has become one of my most beloved singers, but he's also my favourite Cuban historian. He's just one example of something Bruce Springsteen declared years ago: "We learned more from a three minute record, baby, than we ever learned in school."

Good musicians can be great historians because they take us places that only the poets can go. Varela's music charts the emotional landscape of Havana, as well as the dreams and disillusionments of his generation: those who inherited but did not build the revolution of 1959. He performed one of his signatures, "The Sons of William Tell," for the first time in 1989 in the venerable Chaplin Theatre in the heart of Havana's bohemian film world at Twenty-Third and Twelfth Streets. It instantly became a generational anthem, because it imagines how William Tell's son grew tired of being target practice for his dad. For decades, Cuban audiences have sung along to the chorus—"William Tell, your son grew up, he wants to shoot the arrow himself"—leaving no doubt that this is a piercing commentary on the arrangement of Cuban political power.[7] His decision to record a live version of the song underlines its importance as what one Cuban journalist termed "our hymn of independence." On the recording, the sound of a huge theatre singing along builds to a roar when the son tells William Tell that "it was now his turn to place the apple on his own head."

Varela sings about the stuff of newspapers and textbooks: immigration conflicts, the US blockade, Cuban state censorship, and post-Soviet world politics. But he does so with the musicianship of a virtuoso and the imagery of a poet. Unlike Varela's Cuban fans, I don't hear the specific traumas and dreams of my youth narrated in his music. Rather, I have found evocative lessons in Cuban history.

Do governments that rely on direct political censorship produce better artists? I had been listening to Varela for years before I fully caught the significance of this line, which begins the song "Politics Don't Fit in a Sugar Bowl":

"A friend bought a '59 Chevrolet
He didn't want to change any parts, and now it doesn't move."

One of Cuba's old American cars, for which the island is famous, stands as a metaphor for what happens when one doesn't change or update things (cars, revolutions) that were built in 1959. The metaphor hides in plain sight.

Varela's historical vantage point is the neighbourhood. He's the historian of those who observe, experience, and feel, but never seem to *make* historical change. The collapse of the Soviet Union and the economic cataclysm it unleashed on Cuba are recounted in the rapidly changing imagery and fast pace of "Now That the Maps Are Changing Colour," which features burning books, falling walls, empty markets, beheadings, and missing money. "Robinson" employs the image of Robinson Crusoe to symbolize Cuba's place in the post-Soviet world: "alone, on an island, like you and I." "Checkmate 1916" tells the story of the Cuban Revolution as a footnote to a game of chess in 1916 between Lenin and Tristan Tzara: "Sometimes I have a feeling that I was a game piece, and that chessboard was my city." That Cubans are bystanders to their own history, whose main protagonists are elsewhere, is a theme repeated in "Robinson" ("in this game of history, we are only playing dominos") and more recently in "Backdrop": "we discover only in the end that we're nothing more than a backdrop."

Not all of Varela's observations are cloaked in metaphor. "Baby I don't know what's going to happen, if the lie dresses up as the truth," he sings in "Hanging from the Sky"—a song he performed, incidentally, for a million people at a peace concert in

Havana's famous Revolution Square in 2009. Political leaders are sometimes a direct target. In "The Woodcutter without a Forest," Varela sings: "In the region of His Majesty, everyone repeats what the King says." In "Backdrop," he sings directly to the revolution from the perspective of middle age: "I gave you my youth and my heart, and in exchange all you gave me was a world full of stages and silly clowns."

The duplicity of politicians is matched by all manner of deceptions. In Varela's Havana, vendors sell newspapers that announce there will not be a cloud in the sky, and then promptly take cover because they know rain is coming. "There are robbers that hide inside your room, and they hide themselves in our books, in the newspapers, and in the television," he declares in "Everyone Steals."

A decade after the random comment by my Cuban colleague in the film archives about Varela's importance, we produced two books, one in Spanish and one in English, about Carlos Varela. It was easy to find people who shared the opinion that Varela's thirty-year career merited serious reflection, and our book includes essays by Cuban music journalists, US-based musicologists, the former British ambassador to Havana, for whom Varela was a similarly instructive guide to the heart of Havana, and the US singer-songwriter Jackson Browne, who also counts himself as a fan.

There's a funny story by the Cuban-American writer Ana Menéndez, titled "In Cuba I was a German Shepherd."[8] It gently mocks the bravado of the Cuban exile in Miami, through the figure of a small dog that repeatedly declares its pre-immigration glory: "In Cuba I was a German Shepherd." Sometimes I identify. In Canada I'm a history professor, but in Cuba I write books about rock stars. Celebrity culture is increasing in Cuba, as it becomes an increasingly hip destination for US stars. But the distance between Cuban star and Cuban public is not yet comparable to other parts of the world. I learned that the day I met Carlos Varela in December 2009. I was at Havana's Hotel Nacional, having a good-bye drink with my Canadian friend Susan Lord, with whom I teach in Cuba, and Caridad, our Cuban colleague. The hotel's exquisite grounds overlooking the Malecón and the eastern part of the city make it a great place to say either hello or goodbye to Havana, especially in December when it is the headquarters of the film festival and filled with all sorts of remarkably interesting people. For a moment I left my table and when I returned, before I could sit down, Caridad took me by the shoulders and declared: "I have someone for you to meet." She spun me around and I was face to face with Carlos—who is quite short, and was thus literally face-to-face. His music isn't the soundtrack of my youth, but nevertheless it had already made a mark on my soul. I had listened to it constantly since I was introduced to it in 2004, and in fact had just spent the afternoon walking the Malecón, saying another goodbye, listening to him through my headphones. As I stood facing him, a wave of emotion surged as though from the Malecón itself. I was speechless and began to cry. He leaned in, hugged me, and said the only words of English I've ever heard him speak, "Oh, no woman no cry," which made me cry even more. I recovered, began to breathe, and we started to talk.

INTERACTIVO AND EL BRECHT ON WEDNESDAYS

In North America poor Wednesday is hump day—neither the weekend past nor the weekend to be. But in Havana, Wednesday is the best day of the week because that's when Interactivo plays el Brecht. It's not for the faint of heart, especially when you have to get up the next day for work or school. The doors open at 11:30 p.m., and the music starts a *good* while after that. But for those with stamina, it's the best thing going. A Cuban journalist recently described Interactivo's regular Wednesday night performance as "better than sex."[9] On a good night, dancers from various Havana troupes and dance schools show up and perform from within the audience, making the distinctions between music, dance, and sex almost irrelevant.

El Brecht is the Bertolt Brecht Cultural Centre, located on busy calle Línea in Vedado. The main floor houses a professional theatre, where a variety of dramatic works are staged. The basement is another story. It's a crazy bohemian bar, full of rounded wavy corners, mosaic tiled walls, cheap drinks, and impossibly funky habaneros. Almost every night of the week there is someone spectacular here, but Wednesdays are reserved for Interactivo.

Interactivo is usually described as a jazz-fusion ensemble, but even that broad category is limiting. I favour the description of Cuban music producer Darsi Fernández: "They are the sum total of Cuban musical history over the past years."[10] They began in 2000 under the direction of the irrepressibly talented Roberto Carcassés, son of a beloved jazz musician, Bobby Carcassés. The original core featured five musicians. The singers were Francis del Rio, a crazy man from Havana, and Telmary Díaz, a Havana street poet who lived for a time in Toronto. Yusa, an Alamar-born female guitar wonder who now lives in Argentina, and drummer Oliver Valdés made up the rest of the initial group, and Carcassés keeps it all together. At a typical Interactivo performance, there are at least a dozen people on stage. If anyone has seen a sweeter, happier pianist and band leader than Roberto Carcassés, I'd like to know. Their first large public performance was on the streets of the working-class Havana neighbourhood Pogolotti. They were joined by street performers on stilts, who usually entertain tourists in Old Havana, and together they turned the concert into a neighbourhood street party. "It was amazing, like the Pied Piper," recalls their manager Enrique Carballea.[11] Since then Interactivo has produced three discs, filled the famed Karl Marx Theatre several times, and toured the world. They perform all over Havana, too, but they are at their best on Wednesdays at Brecht.

In the patriarchal world of Cuban music, the presence of two bold women among the original five members of Interactivo is revolutionary. That's part of their genius. "Women aren't decorations in Interactivo," Telmary Díaz tells me, noting that almost all the singers play an instrument as well. Interactivo includes the only female conga player I've ever seen in Havana. Mary Paz is a sensation: she strides on stage wearing huge red heels the colour of her drums and her lipstick. The other attribute of their success is in the concept: their adaptability to the peculiar situation of Cuba's musicians. Artists in Cuba have enjoyed, for some time, the tremendous privilege of travel. They come and go with much more ease than do regular Cubans. But the Cold War battleground that characterized Cuban migration patterns meant that even artists could not always count on free movement. The Cuban government prohibited the hip hop group Los Aldeanos from leaving the island for hip hop festivals in 2009, and Carlos Varela was denied a visa to enter the US during the Bush era in 2004, to cite just two high-profile examples on both sides of the divide. Furthermore, the Cuban music world has created a vibrant and savvy audience, but its musicians earn relatively little. Cuban musicians work outside the country for the same reason everyone else does: to earn hard currency. So, Interactivo's musicians move around the world, but they can always rely on their place in the group because of its intentional openness and fluidity. Roberto Carcassés explains it simply: "If you want to have musicians of this quality in a group, you can't tie them to your project because you would be obstructing their own development, right? I tried to create a project in which all those personalities could join in a spontaneous way."[12] For artists like Telmary, who, like most of Interactivo's members, also has a solo career, it is ideal. "In Interactivo, no one is telling me to choose anything. They respect that you have other musical projects."

Interactivo is known more for their sound than their lyrics. People who try to describe their sound invariably speak of their sense of fun or energy, not their message. They are not as explicitly political or observational as Varela, Frank Delgado, or their generation of *trovadores*, and neither do they exude the angry energy of hip hop. But this does not mean they are vacuous. Francis del Rio sings a funny song that dismisses the Cold War in one verse. Noting the similarities, rather than the differences, between Cubans on and off the island, he asks a simple question:

"*No entiendo nada, no entiendo nada. Estoy en Miami, o estoy en LaHabana?*"
"I don't understand anything, I don't understand anything. Am I in Miami or am I in Havana."[13]

INTERACTIVO

EL SAUCE
9na y 120, Playa

SÁBADO 30 DE MAYO

Francis del Río
Athanay
Kelvis 8A
David Torrens
Telmari
Tanmy López
Brenda Navarrete
Pepe del Valle
(Habana Abierta)

9:00 p.m.

★ 87

Advertising Interactivo,
Linea and calle G, Vedado,
May 2015

Taking a leaf from the intense symbolism of the *trovadores*, Roberto Carcassés' "*Que no pare el Pare,*" repeats a simple idea, "Don't stop at the stop."[14] As singer Melvis Santa, who collaborated with Carcassés on the song, puts it, "It doesn't say anything, but it says everything."[15] It's the perfect contemporary Cuban protest song.

That Roberto Carcassés briefly became an international political sensation in 2013 should not, in retrospect, have been so surprising. In October of that year, Interactivo was performing at the "Anti-Imperialist Tribunal" (a.k.a. the *protestodromo*) at an event marking the fifteenth anniversary of the arrest of the "Cuban Five." Los Cinco Heroes, the five heroes, are the Cuban security service agents who were found guilty of espionage in the US, where they had been sent to investigate terrorist activity against Cuba. Their unjust incarceration was a big deal in Cuba; their release in December 2015 as part of Obama's normalization efforts was seen as a tremendous victory in Cuba. The 2013 concert in their honour was packed, and it was also broadcast live on national TV. Toward the end, just before midnight, as Interactivo was winding up their set with an old standby, "*Cubanos por el mundo,*" Carcassés improvised some new lyrics. "I want freedom for the Five," he sang, "and freedom for Maria"—a popular reference to marijuana. In Cuba, where street drugs, including marijuana, are extremely illegal, a public call for legalization is beyond audacious. But he didn't stop there. He continued, creating new lyrics as he went. He sang about wanting "free access to information, so that I can have my own opinion," "freedom to choose my president through a direct vote," and an end to "the blockade and the self-blockade." Finally, he asked, "I have the papers, what's going on with my car?" a reference to another irritant, the system of bureaucratic distribution of scarce motor vehicles.

This was a heady list of issues both abstract and concrete; among the most daring things a musician has said on a Cuban stage. It was without metaphor and broadcast nationally. The reaction was swift. Within a couple of days, Carcassés and other band members were called to the Cuban Music Institute, where they were "separated from the music industry," which meant they could no longer play in state-run facilities, which most facilities are. Popular reaction was also rapid. Social media on and off the island went crazy, mostly in support of Carcassés, but occasionally people questioned the wisdom of using such a significant, symbolic time and place to voice his criticism (which was, of course, his point). Carcassés himself reacted with deep Cuban humour. He released a statement through Facebook that clarified that Maria was a parrot belonging to his upstairs neighbour, who had been punished because she ate some bread that wasn't intended for her. Hence he demanded her freedom. When he said he wanted free access to information in order to form his own opinions, he was referring to his family, who never listen to him when he tells them it's going to rain, so all the clothes they leave out on the line get wet. He went on in that vein, revealing again his creative genius. Fortunately, for Carcassés as well as his fans, Cuban music legend Silvio Rodríguez intervened and the story had a surprise happy ending. Rapping Carcassés on the knuckles for his bad timing ("the struggle for the freedom of the Cuban Five is a sacred flag of the Cuban people that ought to be placed well above other issues"),

Rodríguez nonetheless proclaimed, "Two wrongs don't make a right," and criticized Carcassés' censorship.[16] And magically the ban was lifted. Interactivo released their third album less than a year later, Wednesdays remain the best day of the week to go to Brecht, and Cuban music continues to do what Cuban politics does not.

MOURNING SANTIAGO

For years, people who know I spend a lot of time in Cuba have been asking me the same question: "What will happen when Fidel dies?" I realized in February 2014 that that is the wrong question, about the wrong death. What happens when Santiago Feliú dies?—that's the question.

In February 2014, Xenia Reloba and I were working together in Havana to organize a launch for our book on Carlos Varela. It was scheduled for the Feria del Libro, the annual Havana Book Fair. The Feria del Libro is a big deal. It takes place in La Cabaña, the imposing old fortress that graces the Havana bay. Cuban book publishing somehow remains in the MN economy. Books are printed on the cheapest, thinnest paper I have ever seen, the colours are pretty washed out, the pages become unglued from the spine rapidly, but they sell cheaply, for the equivalent of around fifty cents or a dollar. Cubans turn out in droves to the feria to snap up whatever has been published that year: novels, advice literature, cook books; almost everything sells out quickly. I was proud of how much work had been done to produce the Spanish version of our book, particularly by our Cuban publisher Centro Pablo Press, and by Xenia herself. I was looking forward to celebrating with the some of our contributors from the music studies world who were able to join us: Joaquín Borges-Triana in Havana and Robert Nasatir, a US music academic who was coming from Nashville. We would launch it, appropriately enough, with a concert by Varela at the elegant Museo de Bellas Artes, the fine art museum in Old Havana. I arrived in Havana a week before the launch, having brought with me what I was told was the most important item for the evening: paper wrist bracelets, difficult to acquire in Cuba, to serve as tickets and to help control what was expected to be a huge crowd at the door. The theatre at the Bellas Artes seats only 350, and Varela's fans, everyone knows, can get impatient. To confirm the details of the event, Xenia and I organized a coffee meeting with Carlos and his producer and technical manager, Josué García, whom I believe is the hardest-working man in Cuban show business. Virtually every time there is a musical event of any size, Josué is there, overseeing a maze of cables, sound equipment, and lights—which in Cuba is even harder than it sounds. I bumped into Josué one morning when I stopped by the elegant Hotel Nacional for a quiet coffee by myself. He told me he was there to meet the Minister of Culture from the Dominican Republic who was visiting Havana. "He's a former musician and a friend," explained Josué, "but really the reason I need to see him is that he's brought along a cable connection that I can't find in Havana."

But our meeting was not to be. That morning I got an unexpected phone call from Susan, still in Canada. "Santiago Feliú died," she told me, "it's all over Facebook." At fifty-one, Santiago Feliú was the youngest and I think most beloved of the four Cuban men who defined the musical generation of "Nueva

Trova"—new folk—in the 1980s. Some call the four key players, Carlos Varela, Frank Delgado, Gerardo Alfonso, and Santiago Feliú, "our Beatles." They were second-generation Cuban musical hippies, frustrated by the emptiness of the promises and revolutionary platitudes their parents' generation continued to mouth. Joaquín Borges-Triana famously christened them the "generation of moles" (*generación de topos*) for their ability to live and create underground. Most of them were products of the cultural cauldron that was (and remains) "el ISA," the Instituto Superior del Arte, a beautiful avant-garde art school that graces the grounds of the former Havana Country Club. Decades later, these four *trovadores* had gone their own ways musically, but like all masculine anti-authority figures, they retain a certain youthfulness, even in middle-age. They remain iconic musical reference points for their own and subsequent generations. The death of any of them was unthinkable. Feliú's death registered like a bomb in Havana, in part because of his age, and in part because of his particularly tragic circumstances: his young partner, with whom he was reportedly head over heels in love, was eight months pregnant at the time of his death. Yet his continued youthfulness was also reflected in his life. "*Un hippie del communismo*" was the subtitle of a book about Feliú, a communist hippie who continued to sing tributes to Mexico's Zapatistas and other Latin American movements for social change, even as he criticized his own ossifying revolution. He had a stutter. He maintained a head of flowing long hair. His friends wrote and sang and spoke about him like many do about their sweet, forever young little brothers.

I've never seen a city mourn a counter-cultural musical hero as Havana mourned Santiago. That afternoon, instead of planning

Santiago Feliú in concert. Photo by Ivan Soca Pascual

a concert and book launch, I walked with my University of Havana history colleague Julio César González Pagés to a large Vedado funeral home to pay respects. By the time we got there the family had departed to Havana's beautiful Cristobel Colon Cemetery. The rituals of mourning happen quickly in Cuba. I spent most of the day with Julio and some of his students. None of them knew Santiago personally; all of them were extremely shaken. Julio, who was a peer, tells us all about the importance of Feliú and his music to his generation, reminiscing about every performance he saw over the years. Later that afternoon, a huge crowd assembled on the grounds of the Cuban Music Institute, a sprawling mansion in central Vedado. And for hours, until well into the night, Cuban musical royalty of all ages and from all genres mourned in the way musicians mourn: they sang together. There was a more formal memorial concert organized a week later at the Fábrica de Arte Cubano (FAC), a new club and cultural centre. It was a spectacular and moving array of musicianship. But the spontaneous outpouring of grief and creativity I saw at the musical institute that afternoon gave me new insights into how habaneros maintain such strong connections with each other and the crucial role musicians play in sustaining these bonds.

The people at what was essentially a public wake at the music institute, as well as the audience a week later at the FAC, along with thousands of people throughout the city, weren't mourning a rock star or a celebrity. They were mourning a talented musician who had given them enjoyment and perhaps heightened or evoked some of the emotional events of their lives through his music. In a country where the economic and social distance between rock star and audience is slight, of course some performers enjoy more fame and adoration than others. But that doesn't make them rich, and it doesn't remove them from their world. The currency of Cuban musicians, filmmakers, and other artists is travel, not money. Travel can convert to money of course, and most musicians only start to make money when they tour outside the country. I explain it to my students like this: I've never been to Bob Dylan's house, but I've been to Carlos Varela's house. So if Varela is the Bob Dylan of Cuba, I'm certain that he lives more like me, a middle-class Canadian university professor, than he does Bob Dylan.

So when a tragic, sudden, and untimely death like Feliú's occurs, people mourn him as one would any other beloved, talented person whose death was premature, whether they knew him personally or not. As a poet and musician, he resonated in the culture in a profound way simply because musicians touch people. Without the cynicism and distance that is almost automatically generated when musicians earn impossible amounts of money and/or heaps of fame, the sheen of celebrity culture isn't a barrier in Cuba, physically or emotionally.

To my surprise, there was no talk at all that the book launch and concert, scheduled for six days after Feliú's death, would be postponed. When Xenia and I regrouped and continued working on details of the concert, we went to the theatre at the Bellas Artes to deliver a deposit for the rental (which, incidentally, cost just over the equivalent of $100 to rent for an evening, one of the finest concert venues in the city). One of the museum's security guards was hovering around as we were discussing the event with the theatre manager, and he really wanted to talk about Feliú's recent death. As it turns out they were neighbours, they lived in the same building, and the young security guard was very sad for his widow and unborn child. Perhaps Feliú is an especially acute example of this lack of social distance between musical superstar and regular security guard. The "hippie communist" reportedly had even less money than others of his generation and abilities, and his friends began working to raise funds for his wife and baby, trying to secure royalties for the many recordings of his songs.

As it turned out, the concert and book launch provided another opportunity for the "generation of moles" to mourn and appreciate their friend. To everyone's surprise (including the organizers), Varela invited the remaining "moles," Frank Delgado and Gerardo Alfonso, to join him and his band for a few songs that night. This happens rarely, and the absence of Santiago was palpable. Of course the Cuban audience was ecstatic when the three remaining "Beatles" reminisced and sang together—including one of Santiago's signature songs, a love song *Para Barbara* (For Barbara). But for the little crowd of North Americans in the audience, it was almost unbelievable. We knew what a privilege it was, as visitors, to share what was a moment with national and generational significance. Trying to relate it to my students later, I fell back on familiar tropes of Western celebrity culture. "It was like the Beatles, or almost all the Beatles, reunited before our very eyes," I tried to explain, but that didn't get at it. Some things just can't be translated.

It is instructive to think back on this moment, after the December 17, 2014, US/Cuban thaw, which occurred less than a year after Feliú's death. I have heard more than one Cuban, usually older ones, tell me with confidence that impending US mass tourism to Cuba won't really change the country because "Cuban culture is strong." I grimace when I hear that because it seems like a pat party line, and certainly a superficial understanding of the US cultural-industrial juggernaut. But when I recall how the mood of Havana changed discernibly as people digested the news of the death of one of its "hippie communist" musicians, I think I can see what they are getting at.

"MUSIC IS MY WEAPON" TELMARY DÍAZ AND ROCHY AMENEIRO, TWO POWERFUL WOMEN OF SOUND

Susan Thomas, a US music scholar who writes smart, insightful things about contemporary Cuban music, once titled an article she published about women in Havana's contemporary *trova* scene, "Did Nobody Pass the Girls the Guitar?" It's a question I think about a lot, as I try to understand the often unfamiliar codes and realities of masculinity and femininity in Cuba. Nowhere is this more complicated than in the music world.

Thomas's work details the sexism and homophobia of some contemporary Cuban male musicians she interviewed in the early 2000s, who either claimed not to notice that there were far fewer women than men among their peers, or who made an easy assumption that all Cuban female musicians of their genre, *trova*, were lesbians.[17] It is a bit reminiscent of the way men in the sports world speak of female athletes. Paradoxically, Cuba has a long history of famous, powerful female singers, diva soloists like Celia Cruz or Omara Portuanda (famous to North Americans for her work with the Buena Vista Social Club). So it would be incorrect to say that Cuban women are *absent* in the music world; the issue is rather how their presence is treated or understood, as well as the genres within which they work.

As we've seen, Interactivo is one of the few contemporary groups in which women move from the chorus to the congas or the guitars. Interactivo's Telmary Díaz and *trova*'s Rochy Ameneiro are two examples of genre-busting women in Havana's music world who have moved from the chorus into the front lines, with music that has a great deal to say about their world.

Telmary—who uses only her first name professionally—began as what she calls a "street poet"—rapping rapidly over the music a DJ friend was playing from the stage. "I started just speaking free-style about our realities, our difficulties," she told my students when she came to speak to us recently in Havana. She didn't have musical training; rather she studied literature and languages. Her expansive Spanish and English literary skills helped her poetic imagination. She soon became involved in Havana's emerging hip hop scene in the 1990s. Havana was, for a while, a magnet for international, particularly US, hip hop artists, largely because it was imagined by some to be a more pure or authentic version of the early Bronx days of the genre. There are now at least a dozen dissertations, books, and documentary films about Cuban hip hop, most of them produced by Americans. Telmary laughs about the early days of Cuban hip hop and its relationship to US culture. "We'd all go to hip hop festivals in Alamar (just outside Havana) and the Cubans would be rapping about diamonds and cars. And then we'd all get on the same bus home to Havana where we lived with our parents and grandparents."

Clearly being a woman in a man's genre gives Telmary the keen eye of the outsider and she puts this to great use in her work. One of her most famous songs, from her award-winning first CD, *A Diario,* produced in 2007, is called "*Que Equivoca'o,*" a word play on "*que equivocado*" or "how wrong." It is an angry, yet sweet, girl-friend's lament about her lazy, beer-drinking, domino-playing boyfriend. "How wrong you are about life, my love, how wrong," she repeats.[18] The video, cartoon-like, both sweetens and darkens the message: Telmary, with the snap of her fingers, turns her man's baseball bat into a broom, shrinks him to the size of one of the dominoes he's playing with his friends, and, finally, turns him into a frog. When she kisses him, he turns into an attentive boyfriend. All of this is punctuated by rapid-fire rap sequences that sound, as one reviewer termed it, like a saxophone or a "high octave post-bop Coltrane-influenced trombonist."[19] It is perhaps the single most creatively feminist moment I've seen in Cuban culture.

As well as Interactivo, Telmary worked in Havana with an early hip hop collective, Free Hole Negro, an Anglicized word play on the popular Cuban dish *frijoles negros*, black beans. "It was a joke on lots of levels," she explains, "because here we all were in Havana, which is sometimes like being stuck in a big hole." She decided to move to Canada, where she lived for a while in Toronto, working with Canadian musician and producer Billy Bryans of the Parachute Club, and saxophonist Jane Bunnett. She was a popular fixture in Toronto's Latin music scene for a while. She toured Canada and other parts of the world. She liked Toronto a lot, especially what she saw as its openness and diversity. But she hated the cold and, after her daughter was born in 2012, she decided to return to Havana, at least for a while. She missed Cuba's warmth but also the closeness of family and friends, particularly with a young child. When she explained this move to my Canadian students in Havana, they were amazed. Most of them were just digesting Global South poverty up close for the first time. Even the comparatively mild version they were seeing in Vedado was shocking; they could barely imagine someone exchanging Toronto for the rigours of life in Cuba, if there was a choice. "But really," she continued, "I came back to Cuba because I missed Brecht on Wednesdays." She smiled, but I think she wasn't completely joking.

100

Telmary in concert, December 2015

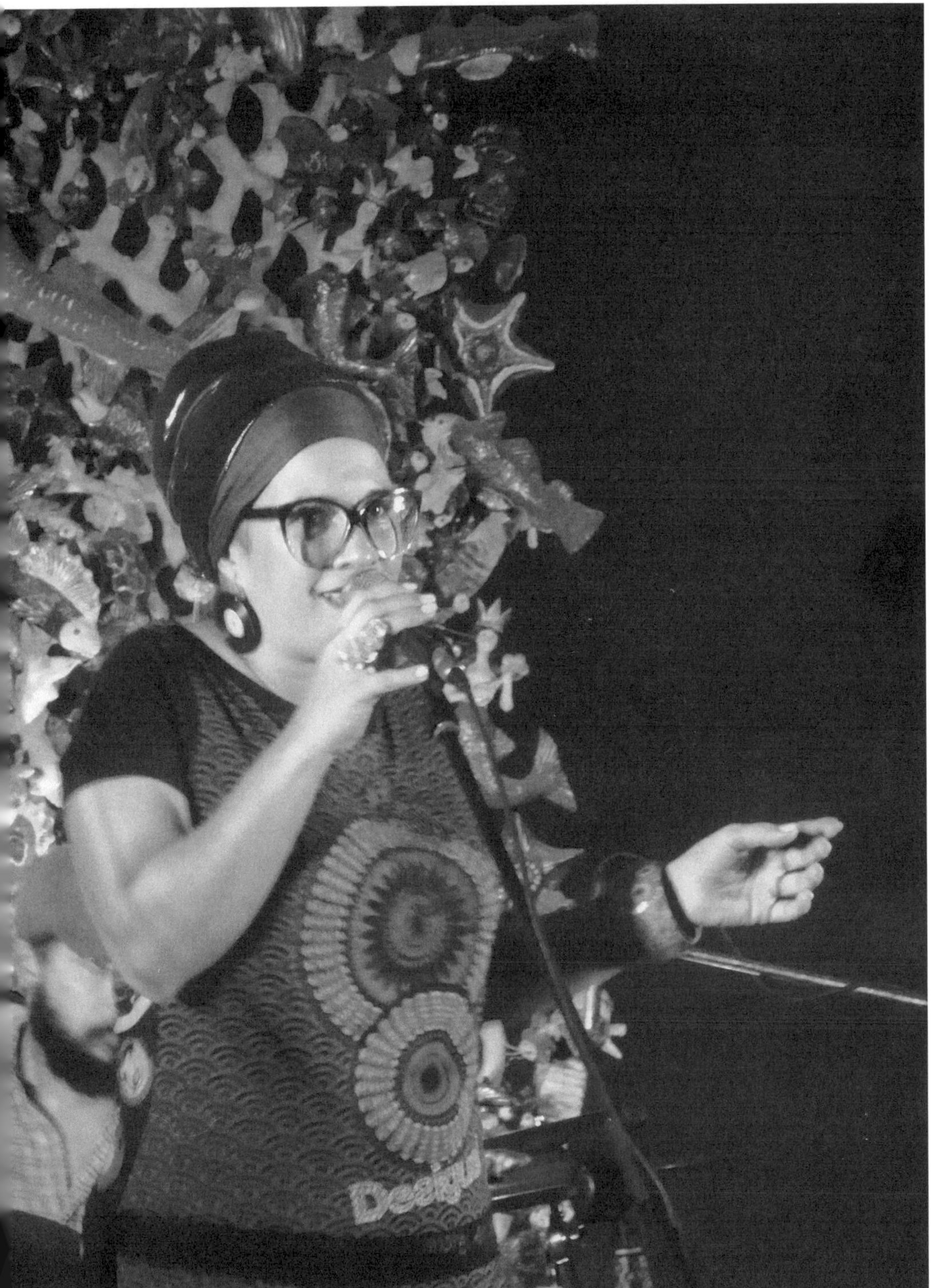

Rochy—who also uses only her first name on stage—comes from a different genre than Telmary's powerful staccato hip hop, but she too is a force of nature. She was trained as an architect and worked in that profession until she decided to make the leap into her true passion: singing. She sings in the *trova* tradition, has recorded three discs, and works with a wide variety of Cuban musicians. Lately, however, she's made a name for herself as one of the voices of an impressive anti-violence campaign she spearheaded along with University of Havana historian (and another force of nature) Julio César González Pagés. Along with a number of Julio's young University of Havana students—many of them athletes who now study the pernicious effects of their culture's stereotypes of masculinity—Rochy now tours Cuba, speaking and singing about violence against women and girls. The campaign, called "*Todas Contracorriente*" (Everyone Against the Current— note the feminine form of "everyone"), has toured all over the island, seventeen cities in total. In a small country like Cuba, that's pretty much all of them. They visited schools and community centres, using music to open public discussions about violence in general and the sexist violence of popular music in particular. As Rochy explains it, "Our idea is to raise awareness through music. Through music you can do many things to improve society, because currently some artistic creations incite violence, even unintentionally. Through music our children are getting a lot of incitement to violence and I really want musicians to consider this problem, and also I want Cuban women to gain self-esteem."[20]

She has her work cut out for herself. Crime statistics—particularly for intimate crimes, such as wife abuse—are impossible to find in Cuba (and are underreported everywhere). Better health,

Rochy Amaneiro and Julio César González Pagés, publicity photo for "Yo Digo No" ("I Say No") anti-violence campaign

education, and employment statistics certainly contribute to a strong sense of independence among Cuban women, which is why, perhaps, there is a common perception that violence rates are lower in Cuba than elsewhere in the region. But, anecdotally, everyone has stories. Rochy is one of a few artists trying to draw public attention to the issue. A few years earlier, for the first time on Cuban TV, a telenovela, *Bajo el mismo sol* (Under the Same Sun), featured a story line about an abused wife.[21] Another brave feminist artist, filmmaker Marilyn Solaya, produced a powerful feature film, *Vestido de Novia* (His Wedding Dress), about the hard lives of transgendered Cubans, which includes a number of powerful scenes of masculine sexual brutality.

But for Rochy, as a musician, the misogyny of music and music videos is the main target. One year, Rochy and Julio brought along a number of recent reggaetón videos to show our students in Havana. I don't think a reggaetón video has been made without at least one scantily clad female adornment to the smartly (and fully) dressed male hero, but those images—which of course we see every day in North American videos too—were nothing compared to the imagery of violence in others. The most explicit was a song, titled "*Se Calentó*" (Heated), by a reggaetón duo, El Calde. The video was like a compendium of urban gang culture imagery: groups of young, muscular black men posing on the street, brandishing bats and sticks, with the occasional shot of a machete (sheathed and unsheathed), and even two shots of someone holding a pistol (wearing an iconic Tupac-style kerchief). The few females in the video were posed butt to the camera, and it all ended in a massive street fight between rival gangs. The lyrics sing a tribute to the fierce men of Luyano, the Havana neighbourhood depicted in the video.

> "The party on the street party is already hot,
> It's heated
> And I'm heading out armed
> If you are brave
> Get yourself to Luyano."

If this wasn't Cuba there would be little remarkable in either the lyrics or the imagery. But it *is* Cuba—where there is no gun culture (some guns, but no gun culture) and scant gang culture, and where men can be crazy macho but don't generally take their fashion or other visual cues from Hollywood versions of inner-city US gangs. This is a country that constantly prides itself on the relative safety of daily life, for both citizens and visitors. It's not that crime or violence doesn't exist, but it is still not a prominent part of the visual landscape or the daily life of Havana. Alarm systems, razor wire, armed guards, chained dogs, gated communities: are all far less visible on the streets of Havana than they are in other major cities in the world, First or Third. There aren't streets one doesn't dare walk down (at least during the day), taxi routes one is warned to avoid, or parks you would be crazy to walk through. Once, Susan and Jordi and I arrived in Havana not from Canada, but from Guatemala, one of the most violent countries in the Western hemisphere. The transition to Cuba after six weeks of Guatemala made for a remarkable comparison. In the taxi ride back to our apartment from the Havana airport, Susan observed quietly, "The only danger we face in this taxi is that the driver might try to overcharge us."

So, it is easy to see why this video was so shocking, and why singers like Rochy place music and music videos at the heart of a campaign for what she calls diverse "culture of peace" in contemporary music.[22] "*Se Calentó*" got no exposure on Cuban TV. But this means little in a country where videos, TV shows, and films circulate rapidly from flash drive to flash drive. Rochy and Julio's group initiated a campaign to enlist high-profile musicians to declare, *"yo digo no a la violencia contra mujeres y niñas"*—"I say no to violence against women and girls." Various musicians have participated, and they got a boost when the island's most popular reggaetón group, Gente de Zona, said from the stage at a concert attended by 60,000 habaneros, "*yo digo no a la chabacanería!*" ("I say no to vulgarity.")

A song in Telmary's repertoire is called "Music is My Weapon." "Music is my weapon," goes the chorus, "but also my defense." It has become a bit of a signature for Telmary, but it applies just as well to Rochy, as she crosses the island singing to school kids: Both of them, in their manner, changing the world.

FÁBRICA DE ARTE CUBANO

A club and cultural complex known as the Fábrica de Arte Cubano (FAC), the Cuban Art Factory, opened its doors in December 2013, and since then it has appeared on just about every visiting journalist's Top Ten list. The *New York Times* included it on its list of "Fifty-Two Places to Go in 2015" and FAC director X Alfonso's handsome face has graced virtually every magazine in or story about Cuba since the place opened. The centre is housed in an old cooking oil factory near the Rio Almendares that separates Vedado from Miramar, at the corner of Eleventh and Twenty-sixth streets. A combined art gallery, performance space, dance club, theatre, and art market, it is frequented by hip Havana art students, alongside their poorer cousins from Centro Havana or Alamar, visiting foreigners, and more than a few people older than twenty-five. It is presided over by a son of Afro-Cuban musical royalty. In all, it's a pretty sweet package. Every time I go I am struck with the same thought: if this were anywhere else in the world it would cost at least ten times more than the $2 cover charge, and pretension would be the overwhelming vibe.

In fact, foreign journalists love it so much they have a hard time convincing themselves that they are still in "Castro's Cuba" when they visit the place. As a visitor from *Punchdrunk,* a US lifestyle magazine, enthused, "This is one of the first venues to realize a vision of Cuba that isn't focused on tourism or reliving the country's romanticized heyday of the 1950s, the last time that Cuba had a vibrant nightlife culture."[23] Of course, it is the epitome of egocentric (and lazy) US journalism to imagine that between the glory days of 1950s American gangsters and Obama's thawing announcement of December 17, 2014, Havana simply went to sleep (awaiting the kiss from her Prince Charming). But how long, we are left to wonder, will it be until the FAC fulfills this New York journalist's nightmare: "If the Fábrica de Arte Cubano existed in Brooklyn, it would be filled with angular haircuts atop skulls filled with cocaine. In other words: utterly insufferable."[24]

With even the tiniest awareness of what happened culturally in Cuba in that fifty-year interregnum between American hostility and renewed diplomacy, the FAC looks a little bit less like an amazing anomaly that fell out of the sky just in time to greet the return of US tourists, and more like the product of a great deal of hard work on the part of the Havana music world. I sometimes describe X Alfonso, the Fábrica's charismatic leader, to my students as: "the Jay-Z of Cuba, but without the zillions of dollars." Like Jay-Z, Alfonso combines entrepreneurial ambition and a musician's creative soul. Both have succeeded despite formidable odds, miracles actually, in very different contexts. X is the son of Carlos Alfonso and Ele Valdés, a creative duo who have performed for decades as Síntesis, a Cuban institution and an Afro-Cuban vocal group combining the traditional, the contemporary, and the spiritual. Both X and his sister Eme grew up in and around the group and both continued on to solo careers. X is a multi-talented powerhouse. He studied classical piano, graduating from the national art school in 1990. He produces films and videos, writes award-winning film scores, and has recorded three discs on his own. His songs are filled with sharp, observant social commentary. His high-energy music calls out to young Cubans of his generation in something of the same way (though with a different sound) that Nueva Trova made the Special Period survivable to the 1990s generation. He sings of the beauty of Afro-Cuban spirituality, the hypocrisy of a society that ignores social problems ("they have snatched out our eyes"), and the power now possessed by his own generation of Cubans. Many of his songs use the chorus as a kind of chant of generational hope and power, in the same way that Síntesis uses Yoruba and other Afro-Cuban incantations. *"Mi Abuelo Dice"* (My Grandfather Says), recorded with Interactivo in 2014, is an ironic lament about the blindness of the revolutionary generation to the realities of Cuban youth today:

> "My grandfather says that in his time, there was nothing to do unless you had money
> My grandfather says that in his time, girls stayed up all night selling their bodies
> My grandfather says that in his time, police beat you up for no reason."[25]

Each statement is punctuated by a long, ironic "umm, hmm." In one song, the revered achievements of the 1959 revolution are turned into the out-of-touch babblings of an old man, who has no clue that the same social problems exist today.

This is all to say that X Alfonso has at least a certain amount of cred as a public figure who challenges, rather than bends to, party lines. The origins of the FAC have less to do with trying to imitate the club culture of New York or Berlin, and more to do with finding a space for the creative cauldron that Havana produces. The original Fábrica began in 2010, and was located in the Pabexbo building, a cavernous warehouse space that houses things like international art and craft shows and the international cigar exposition. Occasionally, the Fábrica would rent it for a combined concert, film screening, and art show, using the huge space to display the artistic riches produced by students at ISA, the art school located nearby. The original, occasional Fábrica became a staple of the cultural scene for a couple of years, despite its out-of-the-way location. When I went there one year with some Cuban friends and a group of my Canadian students, we learned just how thoroughly Cuban the place was: the minimal admission fee was in MN only. Several students hadn't yet changed their CUC for MN and the club wouldn't take CUC at the door. This was the only place in Havana I've seen refuse CUC. Alfonso and a large team of artists and designers searched for several years for something more permanent and finally were allowed to do the considerable work to renovate the dilapidated but beautiful Cocinero building.

Now the Fábrica is a regular part of our course curriculum and Havana's cultural life. The year it opened, X and his team of curators and designers spoke to our students when we visited. They told us about the tremendous work it took to convert the place into what it is, and also underlined, passionately, that they saw the Fábrica as an artistic meeting place or hub, much more

The rock stars and the professors: Carlos Varela, X Alfonso, the author, and Susan Lord, a Queen's University professor, visit to the Fábrica, 2014. Photo by Nicholas Smith

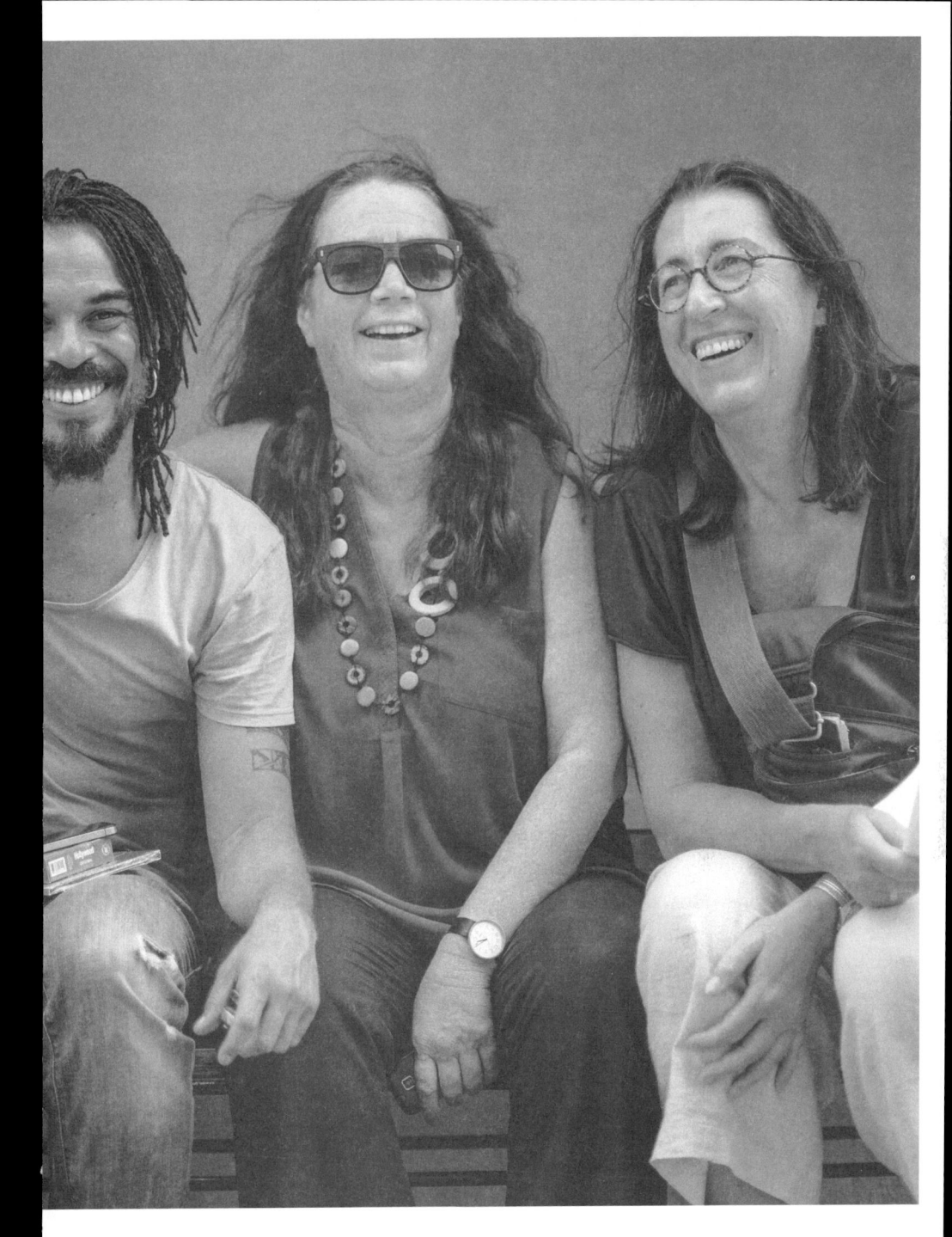

than a nightclub. People stream through to see a host of ever-changing exhibitions of photography, painting, and design, or attend poetry readings or book launches. The cavernous dance club, run by the ever-present Josué García, hosts a dazzling array of contemporary Cuban musicians, as well as the occasional foreign visitors such as New York's The Roots. There is also a smaller stage for more intimate concerts, christened the Santiago Feliú room. Santiago himself was scheduled to perform in the place around the time of his death.

So despite appearances, the Fábrica de Arte Cubano is not Havana's late entry into the generic hip urban club scene. In fact, it is not a private club at all; it is housed under the Ministry of Culture, like many theatre and music venues in Havana. Freddy Monasterio Barsó, a Cuban studying in Canada, is doing doctoral research on the Fábrica and other semi-independent musical productions and venues that are popping up in today's Havana. As Monasterio Barsó sees it, the blunt censorship of previous eras is giving way to a host of quasi-independent performance spaces, including bricks and mortar buildings like the Fábrica, and more ephemeral but regular music festivals that feature a huge array of musical styles and mix Cuban with other international musicians. This is a new level of state-sanctioned cosmopolitanism, and no one knows how far it is going to go. As the chant-like chorus of one of X Alfonso's signature songs, "*Revoluxcion*," goes, "Don't stop the train, don't stop the train."[26]

THREE

LA NUEVA CUBA: LIFE IN THE NEW ECONOMY

CHOPPED VEGETABLES, RESTAURANTS, AND OTHER SIGNS OF A NEW MIDDLE CLASS
The official indication that something was changing in the Cuban economic system started, as things often do, with Fidel Castro. In a conversation with visiting US journalist Jeffrey Goldberg, he quipped—inadvertently after a glass of wine at lunch, or deliberately, who can say—"The Cuban model doesn't even work for us anymore."[1] This jokey reflection in September 2010 was just a hint of things to come. In November of the same year, the government of President Raúl Castro released a document, "Proposed Guidelines of the Economic and Social Policy," which contained 291 articles that diagnosed and proposed solutions for Cuba's vast economic problems. The guidelines circulated and were discussed in workplaces and schools, and formally approved in April 2011. The process of what the government called "renovating" or "updating" the Cuban economy was officially under way.

According to University of Havana economics professor Jorge Mario Sánchez, the changes mark "a decisive transformation in the relationship between the state and society." They do so primarily by making the private or non-state sector a permanent fixture (as opposed to, as previously, a persecuted underground phantom or a barely tolerated necessary evil).[2] The government eliminated some restrictions on the size and growth potential of private businesses, it dropped some of the most punitive taxes and regulations, it actively sought foreign direct investment, and it began to nudge employment from the state to the non-state sector. Before 2010, about 15 percent of Cubans were employed in the non-state sector; by the end of 2012 it was 23 percent, by 2016 it is predicted that the figure could be 40 percent. Self-employment, or *cuentapropismo,* was legalized, with over 200 new categories of employment created—even if the vast majority were things Cubans were already doing in the underground economy.[3] It became legal to buy and sell real estate as well as automobiles.

These changes are ongoing and controversial and there is no end of debate, inside and outside Cuba, about how important they are and what the effects will be. This is particularly so in light of the changes which will be brought into being post-December 17, 2014, and the potential of US capital and enterprises to intervene in the Cuban economy. There is only one thing that everyone could agree upon now: a visible, thriving, domestic Cuban middle class has come out of the closet.

When we lived in Havana in 2004, we sometimes struggled to entertain a five-year-old in a city with almost no children's consumer culture. Cuban children amuse themselves within family or neighbourhood networks. We were often a part of friends' family lives, but not always. So, we occasionally found ourselves, especially on cloudy or wet weekends (or when we felt we couldn't afford the $25 round trip cab fare to Playas del Este, the beach twenty minutes from the city), at Havana's aquarium. It isn't, in my view, a particularly good aquarium, though the dolphins dancing to salsa music is a nice touch. It is also not easy to get to, as it's located in the western-most part of Miramar. On one particularly cloudy day, we headed out by tourist taxi, the only option for foreigners in those years. We got caught in a driving downpour on the way back—a big, dramatic tropical rain. Everyone leaving the aquarium huddled together under a canopy at the entrance and I watched the assembled people turn from a mass of families with small children coping with tremendous rain into two distinguishable groups: tourists with money to pay for a taxi, and Cubans who had to wait for the storm to end in order to walk to a nearby bus stop. Watching myself among the (mostly) white people, scurrying for each new cab as it rolled up, was a defining moment for me back in 2004, but it would not have played out the same way a decade later. Not only would Cubans be among the taxi-takers, but some of them would now have cars.

After the economic "renovations" were announced the underground black-market economy was able to lift its head a little bit, and the city looked like it had rained kiosks. In 2011, it seemed every block included a front yard stand selling something—some blocks more than one. There had been, and still are, small food stands scattered throughout Havana neighbourhoods, increasing in density around the university. Usually they are only open at breakfast and lunch, and they sell an array of food such as pizzas, ham and cheese sandwiches, fruit drinks, *batidos* (milkshakes), and the ubiquitous rice and beans. They exist in the MN economy. Individual pizzas, for example, cost around the equivalent of fifty cents, and thus they are an economical and usually tasty way to have something on the go. Generally there are no tables or chairs. You just stand around to eat and maybe they have a few pieces of paper to slide your pizza on to; takeout containers don't exist. One drinks juice or coffee from a glass that is quickly washed and re-used. Most of these stands have been around for a while, and they clearly aren't easy to open. We shared a running joke with our landlord, Aldo, about our next-door neighbour, who some years ago decided to turn his little ice cream stand into a larger and more elaborate kiosk for takeout food. We watched his progress for a couple of years, seemingly brick by brick, each time we visited. "Any day now, by your next visit for sure, he'll be open," Aldo would predict, knowing that wasn't going to happen. It didn't.

Since then the kiosk economy has taken wings and soared. There are now a huge number of food options and plenty of other buying and selling possibilities on the city's streets. It was discombobulating to understand at first, especially as I realized that what was for sale, beyond food, were basically two types of things: discs, either DVDs or CDs, and brightly painted papier-mâché crafts and tourist souvenirs. In Canada, I live in Kingston, Ontario, in a mixed middle- and working-class downtown neighbourhood, where every summer people turn their yards into permanent lawn sales. The wares are, generally, neither decorative nor useful; one half of the poor of the north end sells their junk to the other half. Those early kiosks in Havana reminded me of the same thing: the entrepreneurship of the poor, who have no access to credit, and no ability to take financial risks. Who was this for? Who was buying? Who was benefitting?

I still don't fully know the answers to these questions, but it is obvious that at least a few people are profiting. I've heard several habaneros tell me they know Cubans who now send remittances to family in Florida; this sounds like a line, but people swear it's true. Disposable income is on the rise, and those early kiosks have become quite a bit sturdier and up-market. One of the first studies of *cuentapropistas* was a report published by the US think-tank Brookings Institute in 2013. US-based Cuban scholar Richard Feinberg interviewed a number of first-generation *cuentapropistas* and compiled some initial data on the extent to which non-state employment has penetrated into the Cuban economy and psyche.[4]

The options for *cuentapropistas* are, as we have seen, controlled by the state. Professionals, for example, are not included; there is no such thing as a private medical or legal practice. But within the 200 state-authorized categories, the most popular choices of self-employment are in food services (including street vendors), accommodations, transportation (taxis and trucks), construction, musical sales (the ubiquitous CD vendors, a relatively easy gig in copyright-less Cuba), and appliance repair. The average investment necessary to start a business ranged from $7,000 CUC in the retail sales field to $36,000 CUC to renovate a dwelling for tourist accommodation. Half of Feinberg's sample of twenty-five *cuentapropistas* got their start-up money from relatives abroad, the other half from personal savings or selling a property. No one relied on a bank (which offers little in the way of loans or investment assistance). Like self-employed people the world over, no one speaks much about their earnings. Taxes, if they are paid, are steep: a monthly license fee and a revenue tax (paid monthly) of 50 percent (after the first 50,000 pesos or $2,000 CUC).[5] This tax rate is not, however, out of line with the rest of the developing world.

This picture of what Feinberg calls a "dynamic independent private sector" is visible every day on the street. I've heard it said that Cubans are the most brand-conscious people in the world — a consequence, perhaps, of being shut out of the enormous shopping mall that is the US for all these years. Designer logos have always decorated Cuban clothing but now they might not be knock-offs. So too the cars, which Cuban men care for with the loving attention one might expect to see showered on a baby. Now, as well as the famous vintage US cars and still functioning Ladas, one can see Peugeots, Jeeps, BMWs, and Toyotas, all at absurdly high prices. In 2010, I noticed the supply at the *licorera* (liquor store) beside the Melia Cohiba Hotel in Vedado had exploded: as well as the customary wide range of rums, their wine offerings suddenly went way past the typical domestic and Spanish selections and began to include wine from other Latin American countries, France, and Italy, at a wider range of prices. Packaged, chopped pineapple and other fruits and vegetables started appearing at the markets.

I was happy enough to see a wider range of wine, though I had already "resolved," as Cubans say, my wine issues when Emilia introduced me to La Tienda de Los Rusos, the Russians' store, located in an old Vedado mansion behind an imposing iron gate. It is a holdover from the days when Soviet technicians thronged

Havana's streets and were privileged, like diplomats, to frequent their own better-stocked stores. Why La Tienda de Los Rusos still exists decades after the end of the official Russian presence in Cuba I don't know, but I do know that if you remember where it is (it is unmarked), anyone can walk in and purchase decent Chilean wine there for $8, a dollar less than most liquor stores. The wine sits alongside an assortment of Russian canned goods and chocolates, used clothes, and, once, a large stack of car tires, all sold by unfriendly Eastern European women. So I was not as thrilled as I might have been at the sight of $9 Chilean wine at the liquor store, but I was overjoyed when I saw packages of peeled, chopped garlic at the markets. Cuban garlic is tasty but tiny, and extremely frustrating to peel and chop; worth paying extra for someone else's labour, in my accounting.

With each visit I now see a jaw-dropping array of what many North Americans would consider foodie necessities. An artisanal pasta store opened near the Galleria de Paseo, which sells artful nests of pasta made from beets, and ravioli stuffed with dried fruit. Emilia found jars of pesto in a small store attached to a gas station on Línea. Telmary introduced me to a bakery in Miramar that makes aromatic loaves of garlic bread. Each of these is a rarity seldom, if ever, seen on the streets of Havana. And then there are the restaurants. Perhaps the most obvious signs of a cash-spending middle class anywhere in the world are bars and restaurants. There are at least two phone apps on the market now for visitors to locate and review Havana restaurants. You can now make reservations for some of the higher-end places in Havana from the comfort (and speed) of the Internet in Miami (or wherever else) before you visit. Other Havana restaurants have banded together to offer on-line gift cards that can be purchased in the US and provided to friends or family in Cuba. The economist Jorge Mario Sánchez told our students that official figures claim over 400 new restaurants have opened in Havana since 2014, although plenty closed as well. The new Cuban restaurant directory *A la mesa* lists almost 500 in Havana alone.

Restaurants, both state-owned and private *paladars*, some good, some bad, have existed in Havana for some time. But the scale of the restaurant explosion would have been impossible to imagine even a few years ago. Most of the time while I lived with my family in Havana in 2004 and 2008, we frequented precisely one restaurant, one of only two or three within a thirty-minute walk from my (centrally located) apartment. It still exists: La Fuente, on calle 13 between F and G. It is seedy in a friendly way, with repetitive food (usually only one menu item: pork steak), but it had cold beer and a huge fountain (*fuente*) in the courtyard filled with fish, which my son liked to play with. We were oddly excited to learn, during our six-month stay in 2004, about a restaurant in Old Havana on Prado, where a salad with arugula and Parmesan cheese had been spotted. Some years later there was a small farm outside Havana growing arugula specifically for the high-end restaurant market.[6]

You can find a little bit of everything in Havana now, including sushi and Indian and Middle Eastern food. There are a handful of glossy new lifestyle magazines published inside and outside Cuba that cover the opening of new bars and restaurants as though they were Paris fashion shows. The days of salivating about a possible Parmesan cheese sighting are long over. In fact, I made a rare visit to a new high-end Havana restaurant, El Litoral, for lunch as I was interviewing someone for this book. There on the salad buffet table I saw the largest wheel of Parmesan I had ever seen, scooped out and filled with grated cheese—as though it were normal, as though it had always been there. I couldn't take my eyes off it.

I haven't made a study of the restaurant scene in La Nueva Cuba and indeed even the pairing of "restaurant scene" and "Cuba" still does not roll easily off my keyboard. But one of my favourite aspects of the restaurant boom is that it provides another opportunity for Cuban audacity. At the busy corner of 23 and G, there's a little hamburger joint called Las PePe, which uses a stylized inverted double letter "P" in yellow as its logo. It looks very much like the McDonald's "M." Another burger kiosk owner near the Galleria in Vedado is even cheekier: Super Burger mimics exactly the Burger King graphic. But surely the award for most creative disregard for copyright goes to the proprietors of StarBien, a high-end restaurant that evokes the Starbucks logo, right down to the tone of green, in its sign. Spanish-speakers will see the double joke, as the name is also a word play on "Estar bien"—to be well. StarBien is owned by Jose Colome. His father, General Abelardo Colome, is Cuba's Minister of the Interior, one of the architects of Cuba's intelligence network and a member of Raúl Castro's inner circle.[7]

There is a funky new tapas bar, Café Madrigal, located a few blocks from where our students stay, on calle 17 near Paseo. My fellow teacher Susan Lord and I decided to check it out when it just opened, as a possible place our students might like to know about. We walked up a narrow staircase and entered a room with tremendous character: high ceilings, huge film posters, and

Super Burger
StarBien Restaurant

original art on the walls: bohemian urban, but not generically hip. It's named for a popular Cuban film, owned by a Cuban film director, and the prices are reasonable (for Canadian dollar earners). It's a nice place, but we debated, jokingly, trying to hide it from our students solely because they would think it was completely normal that a little bar/restaurant like this should exist. You should have to work *up* to a place like this in Havana; you don't just get to *start* here.

A city of 500 restaurants, where the Parmesan cheese flows, the wine lists are long, and the surroundings—at their best—are like perfectly preserved museums, ranging from restored colonial or 1950s modernism to contemporary South Beach. "The entrepreneurial spirit is alive," declared Thomas J. Donohue, president of the United States Chamber of Commerce when he visited Havana in the summer of 2014. He declared support for Cuba's economic changes from a podium at the University of Havana's Grand Lecture Hall, a place of some gravitas.[8] Is this what Raúl Castro had in mind when he announced the economic "renovations" were designed for the "preservation of socialism by strengthening it and making it truly irrevocable"?[9] The best way to answer this question, perhaps, is to consider La Nueva Cuba as it exists in the daily lives of its inhabitants.

TECHNOLOGICAL DISOBEDIENCE AND THE ENTREPRENEURSHIP OF THE POOR

What does it mean for habaneros to live in an economy in transition? It would be superficial indeed to seek a heavy contrast between ruthless "capitalist values" ushered in by recent economic changes and impending US tourism, and the cozy "socialist values" of before. Even if we were certain of what those conflicting values were, and could relate them directly to economic systems (as distinct from, for example, the values that come from families or cultures or religions), Cuba has had a much too complicated history to simply divide it into pre-2010 socialism and post-2011 neo-liberalism.

These days it would be confusing to look to the Cuban government directly for an indication of how citizens are to understand their place in the new economy. Raúl Castro himself can occasionally sound like just one more poor-bashing North American politician, chastising Cubans who "confuse socialism with freebies and subsidies." Complaints about Cuban *pichones* (referencing little birds with their mouths open) have begun to come up in my conversations with Cubans in recent years. Some say the repeated complaints about *pichones* refer not to the poor but to the lazy, and in Cuba those categories are not seen as interchangeable, as they are by the right wing in North America. There is a widely shared joke (with roots in the Soviet Union) that brings the problem back to the low wages of state employees: "We pretend to work and they pretend to pay us." Given the tremendous barriers that the Cuban government has erected over the past fifty years to preserve the state as the sole source of wealth, initiative, and creativity, this change from the language of citizen entitlements to "freebies and subsidies" seems a tad duplicitous.

The spirit of entrepreneurship that so impressed visiting US Chamber of Commerce members in 2014 and the subsequent flood of US journalists, Congress people, and other visitors actually predates the economic "updating" policies. It has its roots in the deprivations of the Blockade and the Special Period. Everyone jokes that the first word of Spanish visitors pick up in Cuba is "resolver": to resolve, solve problems, figure it out. Spend five minutes in a moving vehicle in Havana and you can probably grasp the significance of "resolver": the 1950s Chevrolets still on the road modernized with generations of parts, the Ladas functioning with hybrid motors or brakes, cars of whatever era or model which appear to be held together with tape or elastic bands. Yet they all make their way through the bumpy streets of Havana. As Cuban economist Pedro Monreal observed over a decade ago, the iconic tourist image of Cuba as the land time forgot, where people drive around in 1950s automobiles, could evoke a different vision, of the future, not the past. The image of the old automobile could indicate a tremendous Cuban "technical aptitude" that could be the "starting point for reindustrialization" for an export market.[10]

Ernesto Oroza, a Cuban artist and designer, knows a great deal about Cuban aptitude and resourcefulness. Oroza graduated from Havana's design school in 1994 when, as he explains it, there was no work for industrial designers like him because there was no industry. The stores were completely empty; instead, people were constantly inventing things they needed, using whatever was at hand. Beer cans were used to extend pipes to repair plumbing, metal trays became antennas, a broken washing machine could be disassembled and re-emerge as a fan. The motor of a fumigation machine or a water pump could be tailored to fit a bicycle perfectly. Oroza spent almost a decade crossing the island in search of such inventions, photographing or collecting them. He calls this phenomenon "technological disobedience," which means, as he puts it, that "people think beyond the normal capabilities of an object and try to surpass the limitations it imposes on itself."[11] For Oroza, technological disobedience summarizes how Cubans act in relation to technology, but I think this spirit of disobedience lives in Cuban art, economics, and almost all spheres of daily life.

In 2006, the Cuban government began an energy conservation program, which included trying to replace the hulking 1950s-era Westinghouse refrigerators or equally huge Soviet-era versions with more compact and efficient Chinese brands. This inspired a group of artists, who turned fifty discarded fridges into artworks, painting and decorating them almost beyond recognition. The exhibit, "Monstruos devoradores de Energia" (Energy Devouring Monsters), formed part of the 2006 Havana Biennial and later toured Italy, France, and Spain.[12] Walk down the pedestrian passageway of Paseo de Prado, the tree-lined street that divides Centro Havana from Old Havana, and one can find echoes of this artistic sensibility in the artist stalls set up on weekends: objects made from typewriter keyboards and rotary telephones, beautifully printed renderings of iconic hexagonal espresso makers, prints or paintings made on recycled pages of notebooks or magazines, in which the original imagery or text became part of the artwork. Callejon de Hamel, an alley in

Centro Havana that runs from Animas between Aramburu and Espada, is the site of a community arts and dance project in which bathtubs and other household objects have found new life as canvases and sculptures. Another grand outdoor art installation is Hector Pasual Gallo's "Garden of Affections," a sculpture garden a city block or two long, made completely from found objects, located in the Alamar housing neighbourhood just outside Havana. Gallo's garden was a form of self-therapy, aimed a pulling him out of the depressed funk he fell into during the Special Period.[13]

For one extended stay in Havana, I packed a roll of tin foil for kitchen usage. This is hardly a necessity, but I remembered seeing it once in a store in Miramar for three times what it costs in Canada, so almost in revenge I decided to bring my own. When a friend noticed it, he asked to borrow some to fix his car. Call it technological disobedience, resourcefulness, or *la lucha* (the struggle), or rebrand it and celebrate it politically as "entrepreneurship"—they've been doing it for a long time in Cuba.

REAL ESTATE AS MAGIC REALISM
After the restaurant boom, perhaps the most-hyped change in La Nueva Cuba is the real estate boom. It became legal to buy and sell properties in Havana in November 2011. The effect was immediate. Havana began to look and feel like a Monopoly game, but with almost inexplicable rules. Magic realist real estate: the prices are in one currency but the taxes are in another; title searching is insecure at best; real estate agents are just beginning to invent themselves; and banks don't offer mortgages. Only Cubans are legally allowed to buy and sell (and can own only one

dwelling), but virtually no Cuban earning in Cuba could afford to pony up the money—tens of thousands, depending on the neighbourhood—in cash required to buy anything. How does one transfer, safely, sacks of cash between parties in a real estate deal? When property is bought and sold legally for the first time in over fifty years, how do you know what it costs?

It's not that habaneros were stuck in a fifty year game of musical chairs; there was in fact a thriving real estate market in the past, but it took the form of apartment swapping. The *permuta* (exchange or barter) system was a complex way of transferring properties legally, to get around the strict rules about buying and selling. Parties could trade properties legally, but of course the trades were not equivalent, so a system of evaluation developed. One might trade their small, two-bedroom apartment in Vedado for a larger house in Cerro, for example, recognizing not only the size of the property but the location. One might also include money to even out the exchange, but depending on the amount, that was done under the table. The system was like a giant jigsaw puzzle. To play, one had to have a property to offer. It was an effective but unwieldy and often comical way of moving people around, satirized in the film *Se Permuta,* which follows a group of characters as they desperately try to find swaps for a number of different properties. The best part of the system was the way it was advertised. People would gather on a designated day on Prado in Old Havana with small signs or photos of the property they had to exchange—like pop-up classifieds.

So, a real estate market didn't appear out of thin air, but the initial public frenzy of market relations in Cuba was palpable and peculiar. Overnight it seemed that every second house in

Havana had a hand-lettered *"Se Vende"* (for sale) sign hanging off a balcony or window. Actor/director Jorge Perugorría immediately parodied the moment in a film, *Se Vende*, a black comedy (at which Cubans excel) in which a cash-strapped young woman decides to sell the family crypt, skeletons included.

Some were ecstatic about the changes. Washington's Brookings Institute think-tank termed changes in property ownership a "positive human rights step" and certainly some habaneros would agree, because several have benefitted from the new system.[14] Yet the real estate boom also reveals how, despite all the hullaballoo wrought by the revolution, pre-1959 patterns of wealth and social mobility have changed surprisingly little.

Hope Bastian Martinez is an American graduate student who has been living in Havana for some years, researching a dissertation about daily life in La Nueva Cuba. As housing in Havana changes from a social good to a commodity or source of wealth, Bastian Martinez's research shows how those with better quality housing, in more desirable locations, are able to benefit the most from the option of selling all or part of their homes, dividing them into apartments or other ways of turning dwellings into money. Those who live in these suddenly valuable properties are, she concludes, basically drawn from two social groups: pre-revolutionary elites who stayed, and revolutionary leaders who resettled in Havana to take positions in government ministries. Both categories are predominantly white. Today, the children and grandchildren of both groups—my friend Emilia calls them (and she says it in English) "Mommy-and-Daddy-kids"—are using the capital in their re-commodified homes to, as Bastian Martinez puts it, "successfully re-establish themselves at the top of an emerging hierarchy."[15] To top it off, the state draws shockingly little in revenue from the new real estate market. Properties are advertised publicly in a host of on-line real estate websites in CUC. Yet, for tax purposes, the transactions are assessed in MN, based on the officially assessed value of properties from decades ago. Taxes are 4 percent of the purchase price. So, a $50,000, two-bedroom Vedado apartment (an average price in that neighbourhood, one of the most expensive in the city) might be assessed at $15,000 MN, and taxes paid at 4 percent of that. In other words, the state collects the equivalent of 22 CUC rather than 2,000. There are no property taxes.

My long-time landlords, Aldo and Vanessa, are the perfect example of one of Bastian Martinez's categories of wealth in Havana. Vanessa inherited a two-bedroom, centrally located Vedado apartment from her grandfather, who had operated a successful small business and was able to buy the apartment in the 1940s as the family home. Vanessa grew up there, and when apartment rentals were legalized in 1994, she and her husband Aldo started renting it out. They lived with their extended family in a nearby neighbourhood. Despite a formidable tax system that required a monthly fee even when the apartment was vacant, they managed to save enough to constantly repair and upgrade the place. In a city in which the availability of everything from light bulbs to plumbing supplies can never be taken for granted, this says a great deal. When the rules of the game changed, they were ready to plunge. They traded their own apartment for an even more centrally located four-bedroom apartment, and squeezed themselves—two adults and two teenagers—into a tiny space in the back of their original rental unit. The other family members they lived with (and looked after) were temporarily housed with other relatives. They had two places to rent out (legally, one in each of their names) while they bided their time, constantly upgrading both of them while waiting for another opportunity. It came a year later in the form of two more apartments. So, they sold the newly acquired four-bedroom, and bought two more they are now upgrading; one is small but adequate for themselves and their now reunited extended family to live in, and another, extremely elegant, is to rent out. The last time I was there they showed me, with tremendous pride, the new one that Aldo is still renovating. Showing off the ocean view from the newly painted fifth-floor balcony, Vanessa asked me, "So, is it good enough for tourists?" Then she laughed and asked it another way: "Do you think *el enemigo* (the enemy) will like it?" Now they have their original rental, plus a swanky rental with an ocean view, plus a decent place for themselves. Bring on the Americans.

Aldo and Vanessa are not the Cuban 1 percent. They are not rich and they are not politically connected, nor were their families. They are the very opposite of *pichones:* they work constantly, make personal and familial sacrifices, and they are ensuring that their teenage children continue in school and get as much as they can from the post-secondary system. They fill out forms, pay their taxes, and they don't break the law—or at least beyond what most people do, and have always done, especially in the early days of landlord *cuentapropismo.*

What has given them a leg up in Havana's new real estate world is the simple good fortune of having had a middle-class grandfather with enough money to buy a nice apartment in a central location seventy years ago. Seen from this perspective, the advantages of being white and middle class have outlived all the revolutionary commotion—ideology, laws, propaganda, agitation, education, conflict—of over fifty years.

Housing is one of the most serious problems in the city of Havana. The housing that was constructed after the revolution, usually drab three- or four-storey concrete apartment blocks, relieved Havana's chronic problems a bit. But they created their own problems. "Micros," as they are known because they were often constructed by "microbrigades" of volunteer workers, are almost universally disliked because of what are considered to be shoddy materials and workmanship. Real estate ads in Havana usually start with a reference to when the place was built, and "capitalist construction" is the key phrase that makes a building desirable.

The housing problems people face have multiple sources, but the problems boil down to quality and scarcity. For some the problem is overcrowding. Cubans live in extended families but not always because they want to. Most habaneros still live in the home in which their parents or grandparents grew up. I know several multigenerational families of eight or ten people who live in two- or three-bedroom apartments. Some of these arrangements seem to me to be remarkably functional, but other situations take me aback. Couples split up but continue to live together because they have nowhere to go. People live with extended family members whom they can't stand or who can't stand them. When babies arrive, already tense relations can get thrown even further off balance. Middle-aged people with jobs and kids figure out how to provide constant care for the aging parents they live with. Overcrowding has been addressed by a variety of renovations to fit family sizes and circumstances: houses with high ceilings are divided vertically to double the space, walls are rejigged in living rooms or dining rooms to make extra bedrooms, and entire apartments are constructed on rooftops. These solutions, usually undertaken without regulation and with makeshift materials, can simply add to another already existing problem: the physical condition of Havana's housing stock is disastrous. Roofs and windows leak, and main floors and basements have been flooded so often they retain the odour and other signs of seawater. For North Americans, Cuban sun and sea air are a highly prized, mid-winter treat, but both can be brutal to live with as constant companions. The sun beaming through open windows makes mincemeat out of sofas and chairs; sea air corrodes the paint on buildings surprisingly quickly. Government funds have been allocated to subsidize home repair or renovation, but the help is a drop in the bucket.

Is the real estate boom going to solve these problems? The Monopoly game of Havana real estate isn't only confined to the Mommy-and-Daddy-kids of Vedado or Miramar. A few Havana friends who live in other neighbourhoods have been able to take advantage of the real estate changes to improve their living conditions. One family in Cerro consisting of several people in their seventies "traded up" by moving down. They couldn't cope with their fourth-floor, elevator-less apartment any longer, and they also wanted to expand to have a room to accommodate visiting grandchildren. They found a larger main-floor apartment in their neighbourhood and traded for their old place and a negotiated sum of money. Through the *permuta* system they could have done this before; now it was completely legal. Another person, a single mother with two children, settled a long-standing divorce negotiation with her ex, who now lives overseas, and purchased a tiny apartment. Prudently, she also purchased construction materials to add an extra space for her children as they grow. Mirta spent a few months couch-surfing with friends in order to rent out her place in Cerro to a visiting Bolivian medical student and his wife who wanted an apartment instead of just a room. After she'd made a few months' rent, she moved back in. She's thinking of selling her place and joining up with a Canadian friend to buy a bigger and more central place and share it with what would be a part-time internationally commuting roommate. My Spanish teacher sold her large five-bedroom home and downsized, moving across the street with her daughter to something smaller, and pocketing probably tens of thousands of CUC in the process.

These stories of individuals finding their way, "resolving," as they might say, through real estate don't do much to change the big picture, because the big picture is just so enormous. In 2014, filmmaker Alejandro Ramírez Anderson completed an astonishingly honest documentary about Havana's housing problem, disguised, so to speak, as a music video. He filmed the neighbourhood concerts that Cuban music legend Silvio Rodríguez began performing in 2010. Silvio did these neighbourhood concerts in recognition of the problems that poverty and a poor transportation system create for people who live in far-flung areas of the city, without the means, despite low ticket prices, to attend concerts in the theatres of Old Havana or Vedado. He decided to bring his music to various neighbourhoods, organizing concerts all over the city and inviting well-known musicians to join him. I had the great luck to see Omara Portuando sing with Silvio in La Lisa, a neighbourhood in western Havana. I strolled to a local community centre with Zaira and her mother and there was Omara, the Grand Diva of Cuban music, wearing a blue velour tracksuit. Omara commanded an audience of hundreds from a makeshift stage beside a basketball court. "It was like seeing Barbara Streisand and Bob Dylan play together in the parking lot of Walmart in the suburbs," I tried to explain to my students, but I think this was another untranslatable Havana moment.

Silvio invited Alejandro Ramírez Anderson to film the concerts. As Ramírez Anderson explained to our students after we watched his film, "I realized after about ten minutes of filming that this was not simply a documentary about Silvio, it was also about the neighbourhoods." Silvio agreed, and the result is a documentary called *Canción de Barrio* (Neighbourhood Song), one of the most humane and angry films about poverty that I have seen, in any country. Residents of a dozen different Havana and area neighbourhoods welcome Silvio—and Ramírez Anderson—and at the same time they speak frankly about the condition of their daily lives, and especially their housing. They invite the camera to follow them through their homes, pointing out holes in the ceilings and gaps in the floor and exposing the sheet-metal shanties that occasionally constitute a bedroom. They speak directly to the camera about government neglect and lies and their frustration with the absence of functioning municipal services. All interspersed with Silvio's signature soundtrack, edited brilliantly so that the social commentary of the music augments the visual veracities of the camera. The film has received tremendous reviews inside Cuba, where clearly middle-class people can be just as oblivious to the daily realities of the poor as are people the world over.

After seeing this film, I found that the only thing making me optimistic about what is going to change for poor habaneros is the resolve and determination of some of the protagonists. I watched it at a special screening at Casa de Las Américas, a Havana cultural centre. Ramírez Anderson was present and so was Silvio, alongside a number of participants in the documentary. After the screening, they spoke movingly and eloquently about their lives and their feelings about the film. Maybe the film's power derives at least in part from the *Cubanidad,* the intense Cubanness of the story. The trust that the director was able to establish with his subjects speaks to the lack of distance or social hierarchy between a middle-class, educated filmmaker and his poverty-stricken "subjects." Plenty of the people interviewed in the film explain that they have university degrees and work in professional or technical fields.

When some of the streets of Havana flooded after heavy rains in May 2015, I noticed a similar angry resolve on the part of residents speaking to TV cameras, explaining the damage the rising waters had caused, and especially venting their fury about their neighbourhoods' neglect by municipal or other government authorities. A US political scientist observed decades ago that despite authoritarian political systems, "Silence is not the pervading theme in contemporary Cuba; Cubans have never been silent."[16] But speaking angrily about the government to a camera, this is kicking it up a notch. Making their way around the real estate boom is going to require all the resources they can muster. Centro Havana, the high-density neighbourhood that lies between Vedado and Old Havana has some of the worst housing conditions in the city; it is not an exaggeration to say that buildings come down in a strong rain. Some 230 of them did in 2013, according to official figures.[17] The housing stock of neighbouring Old Havana is also in bad condition (except for the increasing numbers of streets and squares that have been renovated for the tourist's eye). Yet it is rarer to hear of entire buildings collapsing in Old Havana. In July 2015, however, an Old Havana building fell, just off Obispo Street, a central, well-travelled commercial street filled with stores, bars, and restaurants. This time the main-floor apartment gave way, and four people who lived on the second floor were killed, including an older woman, two teenagers, and a three-year-old. Within hours the word was out: the main floor had been gutted and was in the process of renovations to become a restaurant. Interior supporting walls had been removed; one of the upstairs residents had just complained about the cracks in the floor that resulted. A neighbour spoke to a Cuban independent journalist on camera and explained that two "Yumas" (Americans) and a Cuban woman had just purchased it.[18] This may or may not be true, just as the investigation into the cause of the disaster may or may not become public. Another similar building collapse in Centro Havana in 2012 killed several teenagers who had gathered together in a friend's apartment to study for their exams. It was reported on tersely and then disappeared from the news. One of the dead went to school with my landlord's son, who was devastated, and the story spooked us all. A friend who knew the neighbourhood took me by the site of the collapse a month later in order to show me what had happened. In a city filled with rubble and stalled construction projects, there sat a pristine, empty lot, cleared of any sign that a building had ever been there. This was a cleanup of record speed. Said my friend, "They don't want us to remember that these things happen."

TAXI! WHY I DON'T TALK IN CUBAN TAXIS

What is it about taxi drivers? Everyone has a story. A few years ago a story circulated in *The Nation* magazine. It was called "Travels by Taxi," and was written by Elio Prieto, a Cuban writer. He began with his experience in taxis from New York to Madrid, and about what happened when the drivers learned he was Cuban. "Ah, Cuba, Fidel Castro! He gave it to the Americans," was the general response. He wrote a book trying to figure out the tremendous popularity of the Cuban revolution among the taxi drivers of the world.

I think I could write a whole book about what the world looks like from the perspective of a Cuban taxi. Once, I used the formal Spanish pronoun "*usted*" rather than the informal "*tu*" to a young driver who was taking me to the airport. He was so delighted to be addressed formally by a middle-aged foreign lady, he offered me a piece of the pie he was carrying around for his lunch. And I took it (by hand). Another driver burst my initial illusions of what the newly elected Barack Obama might do to end the Cold War. Immediately after Obama's 2008 election, I noticed from a taxi that the billboards on the Malecón across from the US Interests Section were down. No one was screaming anti-imperialist slogans; surely this was a sign that a thaw was coming? I tried to imagine the conversations among Cuban authorities that led to the voluntary withdrawal of visual invective. The taxi driver's response when I made my excited observation that their removal must mean something important? "Maybe, but actually I think they came down in the hurricane."

But my best taxi moment was when I realized something profound about La Nueva Cuba. There are as many different kinds of taxis in Cuba as there are different kinds of cars: everything from new air-conditioned Toyotas to beautifully refurbished US models from the 1950s to the ubiquitous Ladas to others of indeterminate origin which look like they would not survive the next strong rain. But basically, there used to be two types of taxis, whatever the model: taxis and Cuban taxis. Cuban taxis are generally huge old American cars, but not the kind that are repainted and reupholstered in beautiful pastels. Cuban taxis are giant diesel-belching machines—literally called *maquinas* in Spanish—into which are crammed huge numbers of peso-paying Cubans. They drive rapid-fire down the main streets, stopping when you yell at them to stop. And you have to yell because they are usually blaring reggaetón. They don't provide door-to-door service, but they cost a fraction of the hard currency taxis.

And for years they were licensed only to pick up Cubans, a rule that was, as far as I could see, observed faithfully. In the early 2000s, I needed to interview someone in a relatively remote neighbourhood, far outside the central core of the city. Caridad, a Cuban colleague, accompanied me. We had been driven there by a workmate of hers and, as we were ready to leave, I realized we were unlikely to find a tourist taxi to make the return trip to the city centre. We waited as half a dozen Cuban taxis sped by. Finally Caridad said, "OK, screw it. Just don't open your mouth." She hailed a Cuban taxi that quickly stopped for us. I spent the ride eyes downcast, trying to let my hair fall over my face to hide myself as much as I could. I must have looked both ridiculous *and* foreign.

I remembered that image, and the feeling that I was doing something both daring and foolish, ten years later when I hailed another *maquina*, this time on my own in Old Havana. The rules about who could ride in which taxis have relaxed, although the Cuban taxis themselves are still formidable. But I have learned the tricks travelling with Cuban friends, such as how to understand the routes and where in the city to wait for which route. (I have yet to master the hand signals, however, whereby the driver indicates while driving, with the flick of a wrist or finger, the exact route he's taking. This way he doesn't have to even slow down.) I was thrilled at the idea of paying about 50 cents for a ride from Old Havana to Vedado that would cost between $5 and $10 in a tourist taxi. As the taxi quickly filled and we screeched away along Neptuno, I saw that my fellow passengers were all foreigners: two Brazilian men, five young Chinese women, and me. The only Cuban in the car was the driver, pumping up the reggaetón. He obviously couldn't care less who his passengers were.

There are at least two ways to see this taxi story. It could be told as a parable of openness. The fog of a bureaucratic, centrally planned economy has lifted, and as it rises, old xenophobic fears and petty rules fall away. Yet, at the same time there's something missing in a too-celebratory telling of this story. For surely each of us foreigners riding the Cuban taxi that day could afford the $5 fare for a private taxi. Where in the (First) world would we expect an urban taxi ride, even a bumpy, loud, dangerous one, for less than 50 cents? As the cheap taxis fill up with hard currency-earning foreigners, where does that leave the peso-earning Cubans? I spoke about my taxi story with Gerardo, a Cuban colleague who lives in La Lisa, a Havana suburb. La Lisa is two 10 peso taxi fares from Old Havana; if your ride traverses Vedado and Miramar, you have crossed into another zone and the fare goes up another 10 pesos. So when Gerardo and his wife want to go to Old Havana for a Saturday, it costs them 80 pesos in total, which seems a steal at around $4. But that's about a quarter of his wife's monthly salary.

So, I take Cuban taxis with mixed feelings. I continue to follow my friend's instructions of a decade ago: I don't open my mouth, even if I'm riding with people I know. It's my way, silly as it is, of preserving something that still seems to me to be Cuban space.

THE HAVANA YOU DON'T KNOW: STREET CRIME, CORRUPTION, AND *SOCIOLISMO*

I think I have walked every street in Havana, at least in the central neighbourhoods I know best: Vedado, Centro, Old Havana, and Cerro. The only danger I have encountered is the shoes I have worn out. This truth applies as long as the sun is up. At night, what hip hop artist Papá Humbertico calls "the Havana you don't know" comes out. Humbertico's song is directed, disparagingly, at tourists.

> "This is my Havana, the Havana you don't know,
> The Cuban capital after midnight.
> Enjoy it if you're foreign, struggle if you're from here.
> How I love my Havana, what would I do without you?"[19]

Tourists are obvious targets, for envy, ridicule, and also crime. Mirta, who is nothing if not plain-speaking, told me once, "Every time you leave your house here, you scream 'I have money.' It doesn't matter how you dress." But, despite the obvious fact that tourists usually have more to steal, habaneros have the same complaints about crime; they too try to avoid "the Havana you don't know." Of course, in this old adage—the streets are different at night—Havana is no different from any place else in the world. What is more remarkable, what makes Havana different from almost every place in the world, is its relative safety during the day. Most of the Havana crime stories I know are some variant of a purse snatching, which occurs when people (myself included) are walking darkened streets at night. Some involved wallet snatching in crowded buses. Most, but not all, involved no violence, no weapons, and relatively minimal losses. But it's in that "but not all" that the "Havana that you don't know" resides.

This is a Havana that almost no one knows. I've mentioned already that Havana doesn't visually resemble other fortress-like cities in the Third World. There are few visual cues, like razor wire or armed guards outside every place of business, to indicate heavy crime fears. Accurate crime statistics are difficult to come by in Havana; they are secrets guarded as closely as Fidel Castro's residential address. The newspapers are almost silent on the topic, the opposite of the "yellow press" of other Latin American countries, which tend to report crime in lurid and expansive detail. (Of course, they have a lot to work with.) A rare 2013 report released by the national police in Cuba confirmed that crimes of violence were increasing, with the vast majority being the result of personal conflicts inspired by alcohol.[20] There is little crime in the newspapers but there is plenty that travels through *Radio Bemba* (lips) or gossip networks. It was educational to see the reaction when a small group of our students were once robbed at gunpoint outside a Vedado club. It was terrifying for them, even though their material losses were minimal. The police took it extremely seriously and the culprit was eventually apprehended and charged. The fellow had a gun in his possession. But most habaneros who learned of the story believed that was impossible—that the gun must have been a toy aimed at silly Canadians who couldn't tell the difference. As with almost everything in today's Havana, there was a generational difference. Younger Cubans had almost no trouble believing the gun was real; in fact, they had stories of their own about people they knew who had experienced armed robberies. One University of Havana student told me it was possible to rent guns by the hour in Havana. *Cuentapropismo* is a many-headed beast.

Without crime statistics or open media commentary, it is also difficult to get a grip on changes or patterns in crime. Plenty of Cubans say that theft, of various degrees, is endemic in the system. It is basically impossible to live without recourse to the black market, or the vast underground economy that flourishes even after the legalization of *cuentapropismo*. I'm fond of the title of an article about illegality in Cuba by the US writer Dick Cluster: "To Live Outside the Law You Must be Honest." Referencing the song by Bob Dylan (a.k.a. the Carlos Varela of the United States) is the perfect way to communicate the ubiquity of illegality and the porous boundary between legal and extra-legal. Cluster has a concise list of common illegal practices which are widely employed as survival strategies: people sell and buy black-market groceries or cigars or rum or other such goods lifted from state stores or factories; they use state resources (such as vehicles) for their own businesses; they steal equipment of various sorts from their workplaces for resale; they offer bribes or gifts to state employees (to jump queues, or turn a blind eye to infractions); and they sell things that are not to be sold (everything from lobster to charging extra money for professional services). I've seen examples of every one of these categories. Cluster quotes a Cuban friend who explains it simply: "The Special Period will be over for me when I can feed myself and my child just on the income from my official state job."[21]

There is a great deal of moralizing advice in official political discourse about the decline in values on the part of ordinary Cubans, as they constantly straddle the legal and illegal realms in their daily lives. Corruption has obvious deleterious effects on the economy as a whole, but is the informal economy a gateway to serious criminality? As always, the more candid public debate about crime takes place not in the newspapers but in culture. As early as 1991, Carlos Varela recorded "*Todo se roban*" (Everybody Steals), which linked, as a criminologist might, everyday crime to larger social and political structures of power in Cuba:

> "They stole your father's car radio.
> You'll steal his cigarettes when he comes on Saturday.
> And they steal from you when you are watching TV,
> They steal your desire, they steal your desire for love.
> They robbed your neighbour's clothes from the patio.
> He robbed money from the cash register where he worked.
> And they rob you when you are at the counter,

They steal your desire, they steal your desire for love.
They robbed parts of your father's car.
He bought them, at a surcharge, from the same guy who robbed him.
And from you they rob the doormen and the rent collector.
They steal your desire, they steal your desire for love.
There are robbers that hide inside your room,
And they hide themselves in books, in the newspapers and in the television.
They rob your head and your heart,
And this is how they steal your desire, they steal your desire for love."

Crime in the form of bribery and corruption can be well-balanced and strangely functional, a reciprocal system of debts and favours reminiscent of the world of Tony Soprano, without the guns. As a Cuban journalist put it, "Just as we have two currencies in Cuba we have two types of time. Urgency and despair cost money."[22] Those who can afford to jump the queue—at the doctor's office, the market, the telephone company—can do so either by offering small gifts to the right gatekeeper or hiring someone to stand in line on their behalf. When I first entered the Havana apartment world, I learned quickly to keep my store of rum well-stocked, as landlords always needed it to offer a drink to the apartment inspector who visited monthly. As well as my rum (which I started considering part of the rent), in one place I lived the landlord explained quite openly that he paid the inspector twenty dollars a visit to ignore the fact that he was renting us the entire apartment, not a room, which was initially the law. When I shook my head in exasperation to my landlord Ignacio, he took the inspector's side. "Well," he said, "he needs to make his CUCs too," recognizing that the inspector's state employee salary was a fraction of Ignacio's own hard currency earnings from my rent. This is the best example of *sociolismo* (reciprocity among associates) over socialism I have encountered. I think of it as socialism in spite of the state.

Sociolismo accounts for countless examples of petty infractions and violations of the rules. It is how Cubans live. But there are also indications that levels of both crime and corruption are reaching new heights. In both 2013 and 2014, teachers were caught selling the answers to university entrance exams, required by all high school students. After the 2014 incident, six teachers and one employee of the company that printed the exams were arrested and sentenced to jail time, ranging from one to eight years.[23] This scandal was widely reported in Cuba. No one knows the number of students involved, but authorities decided the cheating was so widespread that they also took the unprecedented step of making all students repeat a new version of the mathematics entrance exam. An unreported number of students who were caught buying the exam have been forbidden from attaining university education for life. Daniel attends one of the schools whose teachers were charged, the Vedado Pre-Universitario, a well-thought-of institution attended by plenty of "*Hijos do Vedado*," culturally elite Vedado kids. He told me that perhaps fifty of his four hundred classmates who sat the exam had bought the answers, for prices ranging from eighty to one hundred CUC (more than two months of the average state employees salary). Ironically enough, at about the same time, the US was coping with a similar problem, as the largest education corruption scandal unfolded in Atlanta, Georgia. Eleven teachers and administrators were ultimately convicted of racketeering for inflating the results of standardized tests in the state.[24] Obviously, corruption is hardly solely a Cuban problem, but the scale is giving many people cause for alarm.

Is corruption in Cuba increasing or simply becoming more publicized? It's difficult to know. In February 2014, over seventy paintings disappeared from storage in the Museo de Bellas Artes (Fine Art museum) in Old Havana and began turning up in the circles of Miami art dealers.[25] A year earlier, the Instituto de Farmacia y Alimentos (Institute of Pharmacy and Food), a branch of the University of Havana, was the subject of a serious scandal when methyl alcohol acquired from employees and sold on the black market as cheap rum turned up on the streets of La Lisa, killing eleven people and injuring over one hundred.[26] The Havana Psychiatric Hospital was rocked by scandal in 2010 when twenty-six patients met their death during a cold snap, a result of neglect and starvation. An investigation found that the hospital was receiving funds for over a thousand more patient meals than they were actually serving.[27]

In all of these cases the news was reported in a perfunctory way in the official media, and it circulated like wild-fire through *Radio Bemba* and social media on and off the island. In all cases, high-level officials (including, in the art theft, the Minister of Culture) either lost their jobs or were convicted of criminal offences or both. However, the consequences are no match for the level of popular alienation, mistrust, and horror such scandals have generated. I asked a group of friends at a dinner party in

Havana for details on the alcohol poisoning scandal, which I had heard about but didn't fully understand. My friends explained the mechanics of how alcohol travelled from the laboratories of research institutes to the bootlegger on the street, which is basically a story of bribery at multiple levels. There were three habaneros from different parts of the city and different walks of life gathered at a table that night with Ruth and me, who were visiting from Canada: Grettel, who is a dancer and teacher; Ruth's boyfriend Crispin, a musician; and Emilia, who works in a clinic. Yet the prevailing sentiment from all three of them was the same: horror at the deaths, but also revulsion about what this revealed about the sanctity and professionalism of educational institutions. That laboratory doors at the country's major post-secondary institution, the first university founded in the Americas, could be so cavalierly opened by bribery was embarrassing and unforgivable. The three fields touched by these recent scandals—education, culture, and health—remain the pillars of national achievement. So, corruption in any of these fields, let alone all of them within a few years of each other, is a triple blow that goes way beyond the criminal activities or greed of a handful of employees.

Esteban Morales is a recently retired University of Havana political scientist who has analyzed Cuban foreign relations for decades. He has also become increasingly outspoken about racism in Cuba, a topic not always easily addressed, especially by his generation. As an Afro-Cuban, he lived through the era when speaking of racism was tantamount to a betrayal because the revolution had "fixed all that" and the country needed unity. He has written dozens of books and articles on both foreign relations and on racism; he travels to universities and conferences all over the world; and he appears as an expert on media outlets inside and outside Cuba. But what got him kicked out of the Communist Party, of which he had been a long-time member, was a 2010 blog post he wrote condemning corruption at both high and low levels, which he warned was "the true counterrevolution."[28]

That Morales chose the role of whistle-blower is not surprising. As he told a journalist after his ex-communication, "I was a revolutionary before I was a party activist,"[29] a sentiment he repeated several times when he visited us in Canada in 2015 as part of our universities' exchange agreement. He is a man of strong will and opinions. What is revealing to me about his story is that after a lifetime of outspokenness, the topic that clipped his wings, officially at least, was corruption.

A FEW STORIES ABOUT GARBAGE

> Havana is a city of unfinished works, of the feeble, the asymmetrical and the abandoned. Since the time we were kids, we've been coming across tenement houses daily where cans are piling up and the garbage is becoming increasingly more worldly and diverse.
>
> Alejo Carpentier, 1939

These lines, from one of Cuba's best-known novelists, penned in 1939, caught my eye in 2014. They are quoted in a book about Havana's history and architecture, written by a team of Cuban- and US-based architects and urban planners.[30] I happened to reread the book recently, preparing to teach it, as I was witnessing some of the "worldly and diverse" garbage of La Nueva Cuba.

I had been sitting on a Vedado balcony visiting a friend when I saw a crowd gathered on the street below, peering into the collective garbage container on the street. In Havana, you take your garbage from your house into the street and place it in large plastic or metal bins that sit on most street corners. It is not uncommon to see people rifle through the garbage bins. Usually they are tin collectors looking for cans they bang flat and recycle. Actually, beyond reggaetón or hip hop, the real soundtrack to Havana is the sound of metal cans being repeatedly hit by a hammer. The tin collectors have to practically enter the bins to search because no one separates garbage from recycling in Havana. I saw my first and only public recycling bin in Plaza Vieja in Old Havana in June 2015, which seemed to be obvious window-dressing for the increasing presence of foreign tourists in La Nueva Cuba. In fact, several years ago when a friend noticed I was keeping cans and garbage separate in my apartment, she laughed at me and called me a "true patriot of the revolution," which for her was sort of an insult, like I was sucking up to the state by recycling. (Actually, I was thinking about trying to help the tin collector avoid a dip in the dumpster.)

The crowd I saw around the garbage bins in Vedado that day were not looking for discarded cans of Bucanero beer or Tukola; they had something more impressive in mind. In this neighbourhood there are several high-end stores that sell sporting goods and equipment. Clearly they had received a new shipment, because the bins were overflowing with plastic bubble wrap and

The only recycling bin in Havana: "Recycle for a better life"
Plaza Vieja, 2015

ReCiclaJE
POR uNa VidA
MeJOR

PAPEL

VIDRIO

oversized pieces of sturdy cardboard. Within minutes, a dozen people had swarmed the bin, grabbing up all the useful, worldly garbage they could get their hands on.

I think this was the same visit on which I noticed that something was not quite right with the bins. Usually trucks come by every couple of days to empty them. Occasionally, when the bins fill up, garbage starts to overflow or people place their full plastic bags outside the bins, but that doesn't usually last too long. I started noticing around the neighbourhood that more and more bins were fuller and fuller for longer periods of time. I mentioned it to a neighbour who shrugged and said: "There's more stuff. There's more garbage." There's definitely more stuff in La Nueva Cuba, but there's also less state—or at least a less functional state. In the fall of 2014, complaints about irregular garbage collection— some Havana neighbourhoods were waiting at least two weeks for truck pickups—finally resulted in state action. An investigation into the garbage problem revealed more corruption: fuel skimmed from trucks; payroll records faked; collection routes ignored; even uniforms were sometimes sold. Over sixty managers and employees were implicated.[31] Meanwhile, the army and a handful of volunteers celebrated the anniversary of the revolution that year, on New Year's Eve, by collecting mounting garbage from the streets of Central Havana.[32]

A few months after this, Arturo, who lives in the Havana neighbourhood of La Lisa, sent me a series of photos taken on his walk to the bus that gets him to work in Vedado. There in my e-mail inbox was a series of beautifully photographed images of garbage, piled on the street, no bin in sight. "And to make it worse, this is in front of a clinic," Arturo wrote in the text of the e-mail. We are not in touch a great deal, Arturo and I—we are good colleagues and friends but he's not a big e-mail correspondent between my visits. I think he was just fed up. Photographing the garbage, sending it almost randomly to his foreign friends, was his way of coping with his rage.

FOUR

CUBANS IN THE WORLD, THE WORLD IN CUBA

LIFE WITHOUT THE INTERNET

When Havana journalist and editor Xenia Reloba came to Canada in 2014 to speak to Queen's University students in a communications studies classroom, she used an interesting phrase as a title for her presentation: "How we stay current in a country off-line." The subject represented a remarkable feat of teaching, because it is so remote from the students' experience. Yet she soon had the group—most of them toting cellphones and laptops worth more than a Cuban journalist earns in three years—listening in rapt attention. The various alternative communications strategies that Cubans use to connect with each other and with the world make for a compelling story.

According to its national stereotype, Cuba is a land of long-winded chatterboxes. So it's ironic indeed that its communications system is such a mess. The International Telecommunications Union is a United Nations agency that monitors communications issues globally. It measures national levels of connectedness, using telephone and Internet communications as yardsticks. The agency evaluates 166 countries, of which 42 comprise its lowest category. What it terms the "Least Connected Countries" parallel almost completely another commonly known category, the "Least Developed Countries," and most of them are in Africa. Cuba is the only country in the Americas in the bottom section. In Cuba only 18 percent of the population use cellphones, and 3 percent have home Internet access. Cuba's computer access rates are also low, with seven computers for every one hundred people—the lowest in the Americas. Yet, ironically enough, Cuba receives a great score for the price of its fixed telephone service. ETECSA, one of the few state-owned telecommunications monopolies in the world, offers Cubans the second-cheapest phone rates for land lines globally.[1]

Land line service is indeed inexpensive, pennies a month—and functions reasonably well, for those lucky enough to have home phones. The problem comes in entering the system, because telephone lines are the property of the resident. When you move, you take your line with you, or, if you no longer need it, you sell it separately. To connect a new line to the system, the wait can be interminable, and some parts of Havana—Cerro, for example—offer no new lines at all. It costs between $700 and $1,000 to buy a phone line on the black market.

Unlike most of the rest of the world, land line service is valuable because it is so much cheaper than cell rates. Cellphone rates are 35 cents (CUC) a minute for domestic calls; not exactly conducive to long chats. Texts cost 9 cents, which makes them the preferred method of communication, but here too people are extremely frugal. Over time I have learned that people rarely acknowledge or confirm text messages unless it is absolutely necessary, and no one engages in North American teenage back and forth text chatter—just the facts. Cuban texts are more like an old-style telegram than a conversation. Those without land lines visit friends' homes to catch up on their phone calls, or they ring once to indicate their desire to talk. There's a great scene in the film *Habana Blues* in which neighbours share a telephone by keeping it in a basket on a clothesline that sails between two apartments. Several of my Cerro friends pay their neighbours to share land line access. When I call Mirta, I am likely to hear the voice of her neighbour telling me sternly to *"repita su llamada."* If it rings twice in a row, the call is for Mirta.

Similar ingenuity and entrepreneurship exists around Internet usage—as when, for example, Vivian sends and receives e-mail by opening the window to her shared internal courtyard and yelling at her neighbour who has a home computer. Other neighbourhoods have commoditized this system, creating self-styled home Internet cafés where they rent their connection to neighbours in ten-minute increments. It used to be that $20 could buy you a bootleg Internet connection with a limited monthly allotment. Infomed, the Internet system created for people who work in the medical system, was a popular black-market site. I know several people with Infomed accounts (none of whom had anything to do with the medical system), but these sites are tightly regulated and inspectors often crack down on phoney doctors with home Internet. There are also plenty of people who know how to hack Havana's hotel wireless sites and sell a hotel's access code for an hourly rate much cheaper than the six or eight dollars an hour that hotels charge their patrons. Antonio, a University of Havana student, explained how he and his friends bring their phones or laptops (the few who have them) to streets close to the big Havana hotels in order to maximize the signal strength. One of the hacker programs that opens the locked tourist Wi Fi is called "Your Freedom," which echoes the name of a program that technologically overwrought North Americans can use to lock themselves out of Google or Facebook temporarily.

In 2014, ETECSA began offering a new service called Nauta, which provides limited Internet access via cellphones. A Nauta connection is cheap, only a couple of dollars, and e-mail messages cost one cent to send or receive. In July 2015, a number of WiFi hotspots opened in central locations in Havana. At a price of two dollars an hour, this is the cheapest way to navigate the Internet in the country. It is a fraction of hotel WiFi rates. Yet two dollars an hour is still almost a day's pay for a state employee and the service itself is slow and frustrating. When ETECSA opened its cellphone Internet service, its already strained infrastructure groaned almost audibly under this new weight of users. Dannys, who works in the arts and has a number of international associates with whom she needs to maintain contact, told me that since Nauta was created, she does all her e-mail business before 6 a.m. Otherwise the lines are hopelessly clogged and she can't log in. When it rains, cellphone service goes wonky. Even the more reliable land line service is susceptible to strange things. I couldn't reach Ines for a few days. She finally explained that her land line service got scrambled after fierce rains hit the city and did something to the phone service, even though she lives miles away from where flooding had occurred. That was in May, over Mother's Day, and a neighbour three blocks away kept trudging over to her place to convey the many Mother's Day greetings she received from friends and family all over the world that were somehow ringing in on his line.

The entrepreneurship of the poor that is evident in the kiosk capitalism of Havana's streets is obvious too in the rocky communications system. Revolico.com is an on-line classified advertisement system that was started by students at Havana's polytechnic university. The Craig's List or Kijiji of Cuba, it features everything from real estate to lawn chairs.[2] In Canada, a group of Cuban immigrants, working with friends still on the island, began a website called "Havana Street View." It is a creative alternative to Google Maps—which as a US enterprise obviously does not exist in Cuba.[3]

But the mother of all technologically disobedient Cuban initiatives has to be el Paquete Semanal. The US media have referred to "the weekly package" as "the Google of Cuba," but I think the designation by Cuban intellectual Victor Fowler—"the Internet of the poor"—is more accurate.[4] It's a mix of Google, Netflix, TV, and Kijiji, delivered to your door on flash drives. Pamela, a Canadian I know, happened to be visiting Havana friends at their home when el Paquete arrived. "It's like Christmas comes, weekly," she told me. For a dollar or two, el Paquete provides the latest international TV shows, films, and sports events. Some versions include newspapers and magazines. The source is largely US programming, though Latin American material is also available. Every el Paquete also includes local classifieds, such as apartment listings and restaurant ads. Distributors go door to door and download the package onto home computers or TVs, or, for an additional fee, they leave the drive, returning a few days later with a new supply. According to one of the inventors of the system, recently the subject of a laudatory interview in *Forbes* magazine, el Paquete has been successful not only because it fills a great demand, but because it relies on the enthusiasm of distributors who make money from sales or rentals. Elio Hector Lopez, one of el Paquete's founders, explained to *Forbes* that some distributors are making more money than el Paquete's creators, because they have expanded their customer base like wildfire; which, he says, is fine with him.[5]

All of this technological creativity can be fairly awesome to behold, but as with other kinds of entrepreneurship, it is always wise to keep the limitations in view. When individual cellphones first became available they were permitted for foreigners only. Cubans got around this, as they did in the old days when only foreigners could buy in tourist shops, by asking friends for help. During one visit in 2008, I drove with Aldo and Vanessa to the grandly named Miramar Trade Center one afternoon to line up at the ETECSA office and buy myself a cellphone line. I uttered not a word during the exchange. Vanessa and the ETECSA clerk, in plain view of an office full of waiting Cubans, negotiated the whole thing. I showed my passport, signed where necessary, and handed over the cash (which Vanessa had given me in the car). We laughed about the ridiculousness of the situation on the way home, but at one point Vanessa got serious. "Look," she said, "they put all this money into educating us so well, and then they treat us like children. How crazy is that?" I continue to watch my Canadian students consider how they might survive as students with the 150-megabyte monthly Internet allowance that their Cuban counterparts receive at the University of Havana. An hour on Facebook alone might swallow up almost a quarter of that. I observe Cuban colleagues when visiting Canada soak up the high-speed WiFi at my house or university office with the same intensity that Canadians soak up the Cuban sun in February. I see Cubans in Canada trying to stay in touch with their loved ones on the island with no Skype, little e-mail, and phone calls that can run two dollars a minute. Vanessa is correct: All of the education has led to a tremendous level of inventiveness, but it's not solely technological. It relies on relationships and community. Imagine where else this ingenuity could go.

THE DRAMA OF THE SUITCASES: HOW TO SMUGGLE A SALMON INTO HAVANA

If I were to add up the list of things that I, my family, my students, and fellow teachers have brought along to Havana, it would fill a warehouse, or at least a paragraph. We repeatedly tell our students that they, for two weeks, are going to live and learn in a country that does not have a consumer economy. But like the Internet or the air, the absence of ready, constant shopping is a bit much for twenty-year-old Canadians to imagine until they get there. I must admit that even after ten years of regular visits, it is for me too. As my Canadian friend Ruth put it sardonically, in Cuba every day is "Buy Nothing" day.

Stores that sell consumer goods are located in the scant malls and shopping streets around the city. A few stores sell hardware, auto parts, furniture, domestic appliances, books, toys, and clothing. As well as the malls, Obispo, a long-time shopping street in

Old Havana, caters to both the tourist and the habanero market. Just between Centro and Old Havana, Galiano Avenue (a.k.a. Italia, a name rarely used), the street that used to house several of Havana's 1950s-era department stores, remains a busy shopping street. I have noticed improvements in the variety and quality of some things in Havana's stores over the last ten years. Clothes in the stores are poor quality and expensive, but the clothes, shoes, and handbags in various small craft markets around the city are great. There is a terrific handmade shoe market in Vedado (at calle Primero and D street), and another one in the small craft market on Obispo in Old Havana. There are also extremely good art and craft exhibitions held occasionally in the Pabellon on La Rampa and in the Pabexpo Exhibition Complex further afield. In December, an international art and craft market in the Pabexpo features an overwhelming array of artistry. High-end furniture design is on the rise in Havana, and the work is both expensive and beautiful.

Yet in all the stores, whatever the quality or availability of the goods, prices are near impossible in relation to the level of Cuban salaries. Generally, things, almost all things, are in the same range as in Canada, and many are much more expensive. Given that a bottom-end electric fan costs well over a month's salary, Cubans not surprisingly have a vexed and complicated relationship to shopping. Stores and malls are busy places; habaneros like to shop as much as anyone else. But stores themselves are not the first or last go-to place for finding that necessary something. People find things—from plumbing supplies to matches and brooms—through various other means. Some are legal, some less so; some are visible (broom vendors regularly walk the streets of Havana), some require a labyrinth of friends, contacts, and local knowledge that few visitors possess. The underground consumer economy is so strong it is often the case that the vendors gathered outside the Galleria mall on Paseo, or around the corner from the Carlos Tercera complex, for example, offer more useful products, at better prices, than do the stores inside.

People also get things from family and friends who visit from outside the country. Plenty of Canadian tourists tell stories of friendships they have developed with hotel staff they've come to know over years of visits, for whom they regularly bring vitamins or other necessities. Preparations for my own visits have become routine. We call it the *drama de las maletas*, the drama of the suitcases. My son jokes that we barely need a scale any longer to judge when the suitcases have reached the magic figure of twenty-three kilos, the airlines' weight limit. When Jordi was younger and we were going for extended periods, packing had to include a wide range of child-related medicines and amusements. These days we are more focused on gifts for and requests from friends. Camomile tea, vitamins, baby wipes, eye drops, latex-free Band Aids, sheets, all manner of children's medicine, hot sauce, allergy pills, data storage cards for phones or cameras, toothpaste, light bulbs, deodorant, scrub brushes, spices, inner tubes for automobile tires, a bicycle tire, and printer cartridges come to mind as specific necessities people have requested. Sometimes friends ask for bigger ticket items they insist on paying for—laptops, a computer monitor, external drives, once, memorably, a baby carrier. Xenia once asked me to investigate the cost of transporting an Akita puppy by air—a friend of hers in Havana had a lifelong dream of owning one.

The conversation went no further when I reported the price, which ran in the hundreds of dollars (before the price of the dog). Of course, we also bring gifts, which over the years have also settled into familiar categories: items from the world of food, children, and school. Aged Canadian cheddar cheese is always really popular, and surprisingly easy to transport.

There is inevitably a moment, sometimes more than one, in pre-Havana preparations when all this packing seems sad, surreal, and futile. I hesitate to ask Cuban friends the question, "What do you need?" because it is so ridiculous and my contribution seems the very definition of a drop in a bucket. I am gratified when people ask me directly for things they need. This has become part of the fabric of reciprocal friendships in vastly unequal circumstances. But I am also fully aware that when people ask for tea or scrub brushes or cough syrup, they are conscious of my capacities, financially and physically.

A great deal of frustration and emotion about the geopolitics of underdevelopment, empire, and the Cold War is attached to every container of vitamins we carefully weigh in our suitcases. There is drama every step of the way: worrying about airline weight limits, and then worrying about what the Cuban customs agents will make of our strange luggage assortment. Generally Cuban customs receives visiting Canadians more graciously than they do returning Cubans. One time, two of my students were stopped for an hour while Havana customs officers tried to make sense of the two suitcases of medical supplies we had brought as donations from a Canadian NGO (actually we had brought three — one got through without incident). Rather than face another hour of Cuban donation bureaucracy, we left them there, which may have been their goal. From that experience we learned never to put a whole lot of the same thing in one suitcase. Another time, I had to convince a customs agent that a student was bringing a large box of paper clips as a donation to the university (another random donation from an NGO in Canada) rather than intending to sell them on the street herself. But because we've been so brazen in bringing such a strange assortment of things for so long, Cuban customs agents no longer scare me.

One December holiday visit, we decided to surprise our friends with as Canadian a gift as we could imagine: a fresh salmon. We froze it and wrapped it carefully in newspaper and tin foil. This was back when Jordi was quite young and, as many travelling parents know, you can get almost anything across a border if you have a sweet-faced child at your side. However, we hadn't counted on the airline chaos that often occurs in December. One piece of our luggage didn't make the sold-out flight, and, as luck would have it, it was the salmon suitcase. We tried to imagine the disgusting smelly mess that would arrive, not to mention the reprimand from Cuban authorities. But instead, the suitcase arrived intact two days later, with the salmon still partially frozen. We had a fine New Year's Eve feast in Vedado that year; ten years later Aldo still tells that story, shaking his head at our audaciousness. My nervousness about crossing borders was vanquished forever.

TAKING CUBANS TO COSTCO

I am standing with Joaquín Borges-Triana in Kingston's Walmart store. He and Xenia Reloba are both in Canada to give lectures to Canadian students and celebrate the publication of the book about Carlos Varela that we worked on together. We are waiting for Xenia and Zaira, a Cuban student at Queen's, to find something Xenia had just remembered was on her shopping list. As stressful and anxiety-producing as the *drama de las maletas* can be when it comes to packing and transporting them, it can be pretty fun to fill suitcases headed for Havana, particularly while shopping in the company of Cubans. The agreement my university has with the University of Havana is at least partially reciprocal: we send thirty students annually for our course, and we host one Cuban academic or artist in Kingston for a couple of weeks. Over almost ten years of hosting Cuban academics and artists in Canada, I've enjoyed plenty of shopping trips like this. Stores such as Costco and Walmart are places I try to avoid, but I permit myself what I call the Cuban exception: I go only when accompanied by visiting Cubans. It is indeed a peculiar aspect of my professional life that I can say proudly that I have accompanied some of Havana's foremost intellectuals, writers, and filmmakers to the big box stores of suburban Kingston, Ontario.

It's instructive to shop with visiting Cubans because, in my experience, they are just as blown away by North American consumer culture overdrive as my Canadian students in Havana are by Cuban consumer "underdrive." They are serious shoppers — in Canada as much as at home — but they have a keen eye for the vast ridiculousness of what fills our stores. Imagine, for example, explaining that the aisles of stuffed toys in a pet store are not actually meant for Canadian children, but intended as toys for dogs and cats. Cubans are also, to generalize, friendly and outspoken with Canadian store clerks. I've watched in amusement as my visiting colleagues first pester, then charm the sales staff, many of whom have enjoyed a short visit to Varadero or other Cuban beaches and are delighted to speak to a Cuban in Kingston. Our shopping trips together tend to be really funny and allow me to reflect on my world through an outsider's eye—which is, perhaps, why Joaquín's question in Walmart that day catches me off-guard. "Ah, Karen," he says, "you know Cuba better than many foreigners. Do you think we'll ever be a normal country?" He is part joking and part wistful, but I still can't tell the proportions of each.

Mobile Cubans are advantaged Cubans, but there are liabilities that accompany visas and passports. Cubans who live abroad and return for a visit used to be stock buffoonish characters in Cuban popular culture. There's a dreadfully didactic 1986 film, *Lejania* by Jesus Díaz, about a Cuban family separated by immigration conflicts. The wickedness of the mother—who left her son behind when she moved to Florida—is underscored by her bulging suitcases as she returns to visit. All the jeans and toys in the world cannot redeem her. Cubans who left the island in the decades after the revolution were derided as *gusanos* (worms), because when you left the revolution you left the nation (and vice versa). Today, huge suitcases for sale on the streets of Miami are now mockingly termed *"gusano* bags," an ironic reference to the importance of what the bags contain when they now arrive, filled, in Cuba. Frank Delgado has a beautiful song, *"La Otra Orilla"* (The Other Shore), that parodies those bitter days of immigration conflicts, heaping particular scorn on those Cubans—like him—who remained on the island and cursed their friends and family for leaving. "They didn't say *gusano* any more," he sings about his Miami uncle, because upon his return he had become a "communitarian," another reference to the importance of remittances and gifts from outside Cuba.[6] Those bitter days of migration conflicts are mostly over. Cuba relaxed some of its rigid rules in 2013 which had made leaving difficult, and nobody yells *traidores* (traitors) at Cubans who leave. But vestiges of mean-spiritedness toward mobile Cubans remain, in the complicated regulations facing Cubans returning from longer periods abroad (in the form of visa and luggage charges) and in the nastiness of many customs officials, who, I am told, treat returning Cubans extremely badly, even if they have just been away for a short visit.

I hate Walmart, and I'm still a critic of North American over-consumption. But years of taking Cubans shopping have cured me of any moralistic notions I once had about the nobility of deprivation. I understand what Joaquín's question about the potential for "normalcy" in Cuba means, I think, when I consider what my Cuban colleagues purchase during their rare North American shopping trips. Their lists are not unlike my own pre-departure list of requests Cuban friends have made, but even more particular and intimate. I've helped two colleagues find good quality non-synthetic socks for family members with foot problems. Another spent most of her honorarium from her lectures at Queen's on expensive orthopedic shoes for her young daughter. One friend bought a dozen simple cloth shopping bags, gifts for each of her child's teachers in primary school. Others return with boxes of couscous or quinoa or rice crackers; things we've served them in Canada that aren't available in Havana, and they want to share them with family members there. These shopping trips are hardly extravagant buying frenzies. Rather, they fill immediate needs and provide small pleasures. I sometimes try to nudge friends into buying things for themselves that have caught their eye, usually to no avail. The advantage of travel is something to be shared, even in tiny increments.

THE THERMOMETER THAT STRUCK UP MY MOST UNUSUAL FRIENDSHIP

Before I started spending time in Havana, I was, for many years, a Canadian tourist in Varadero. I spent Christmas of 2000 there with my family and my sister's family. A Queen's colleague asked me to bring something to a friend connected to the University of Havana and gave me the telephone number of two contacts. I called one of them and we made a plan to meet up in a central location in Old Havana during a day trip we planned to make from the beach.

We enjoyed a beer and French fries together in a restaurant in Old Havana one afternoon. Ines admired the young Jordi, then an adorable one-year-old. I handed over the package we had been charged with delivering. It was a small thermometer wrapped in a resealable plastic bag and a small manila envelope. Ines, a philosophy professor at the University of Havana, was grateful we had delivered it, and explained it was for the young son of a colleague, another philosophy professor. The son was six years old, she told us, susceptible to frequent colds. The family will be really happy to have this, she said.

Some fifteen years later I was gathered with my family at the dining-room table of my colleague Lourdes, another University of Havana philosophy professor. At the table in her Vedado apartment was her son Dairon, a handsome twenty-one-year-old and one of my best friends in Havana. We were idly speaking about our long-standing family friendship and our various visits, and I suddenly remembered the thermometer story. Until then I had never really thought further about who the thermometer was for. "Are you the family we once brought a thermometer for?" I asked, starting to connect some old dots. Lourdes smiled and silently left the table. She returned with the same manila envelope, the same resealable plastic bag, containing the same thermometer. It still works and it's now an important part of the family medical kit for the recently arrived granddaughter.

These kinds of stories are fun in any circumstances among any group of people who find they are connected through little moments of chance that sometimes grow into relationships. Another Cuban/Canadian gathering at another dining-room table, this time in Canada, produced a similar random but powerful story of connection. Zaira, a Cuban student at Queen's, was living in our house in Canada while we were in Havana. Marcel Beltrán, a Cuban filmmaker visiting Canada, was passing through town and stopped to visit her for dinner. He looked up from his meal, noticed a small painting on our wall, and his eyes filled with tears. "My mother painted that," he said. I had bought the beautiful painting of a crab, one of Jordi's favourite things to chase on the beach, in a small tourist shop in Old Havana the year before.

What the thermometer story illustrates to me is that each package delivered or item purchased and transported to Cuba enters a web of relationships and exchanges that can, if the circumstances are right, generate something that goes way beyond the value of the item itself. It is a story that makes more intelligible the origins of my friendship with Dairon, a twenty-one-year-old

Afro-Cuban male—an unusual pairing. Our friendship has grown, since our unwitting thermometer connection, because of our mutual love of contemporary music. I often introduce Dairon as my professor of Cuban Cultural Studies. He calls us his *Modern Family* (the US TV show featuring a gay couple with an adopted child that he knows from el Paquete). We go to concerts together in Havana and he is single-handedly responsible for a good part of my Cuban musical education. In exchange, I help him expand his English vocabulary beyond what he learned from his first teachers, Kanye West and Jay-Z. My son venerates him as an older, hipper brother, and now generations of my students spend time with him and his friends and negotiate their own friendships across borders. We keep in sporadic touch through Facebook when he can succeed in finding an Internet connection, and when something really big in Havana is going on Dairon texts me a brief report. "I am the happiest man in Havana today," he texted a while ago. "I just saw Beyoncé and Jay-Z on the street."

Boundaries and differences like ours are possible to cross at home, too. But there is something in the nature of this friendship that seems emblematically Cuban to me, perhaps because it began by a combination of a simple gift and multiple relationships.

LOOKING FOR THE ENEMY IN MANHATTAN: HOW MY FRIEND EMILIA ENDED THE COLD WAR

On the morning of Wednesday, December 17, 2014, I was in Havana, walking to an appointment at an office in Miramar. I had been in Cuba for a couple of weeks; I had just come back to Havana from an intense time in eastern Cuba. I had accompanied Ines Rodríguez to that part of the island on a visit we had planned for a long time: retracing her steps from when she was a teacher in the 1961 literacy campaign. She hadn't returned since that time and she was really keen to see the legacies of the time she spent there, teaching people to read when she was just sixteen years old. I felt blessed that I could accompany her and we experienced some remarkable moments trudging up mountains interviewing former students and teachers. Eastern Cuba, or *"Oriente,"* is known as the cradle of the revolution, the place where it all began. My savvy Havana friends warned me I was in for a world of more ideological rigidity than I had become accustomed to in relatively cosmopolitan Havana. They did not exaggerate. When I arrived back in Havana after our time in rural *Oriente,* I was still reeling. Most of the people we spoke with were enthusiastic and warm and spoke from the heart. But we had endured some really didactic, doctrinaire discussions with local officials—the kind of people I am generally able to avoid in Havana. One local history functionary gave us a long speech about how awful it was that the *"bandera del enemigo,"* the enemy's flag, was arriving in Cuba through the current fashion for stars-and-stripes-themed T-shirts and other adornments. I felt like I had stepped back in time, at least a couple of decades.

All this made the announcement of US/Cuban rapprochement that day even more of a surprise. I heard about what was unfolding as I was heading to the Miramar offices of CARE Canada, one of the few Canadian NGOs in Cuba. I had an appointment with Christina Polzot, their dynamic director in Cuba whom I had met briefly before. I wanted to invite her to speak to our students when we were next in Havana. As I approached their office, my cellphone rang. I saw it was Emilia calling, which was strange for several reasons. I was staying with her and had seen her at breakfast a couple of hours ago. And Cubans text, they rarely call, due to the crazy phone rates. I answered and her first words were, "Did you hear the news?" My first thought was "Fidel died," which was immediately followed by, "No, Emilia sounds happy. She probably would not sound so thrilled to announce someone's death." Of course, she was calling to tell me that Cuba and the US were swapping political prisoners — Allan Gross, the American, for the so-called Cuban Five (who were now four as one had already been released) — and that Barack Obama and Raúl Castro were scheduled to make speeches shortly. I said something like, "Wow, this might be it," and Emilia agreed, though I now wonder what we thought "it" was exactly.

I continued to the CARE office and spoke to Christina. Our meeting was punctuated, however, by the constant sound of our cellphones receiving messages from friends in Canada and in Cuba about the unfolding events. Christina's husband, Stephen Wickery, is a Canadian journalist who was extremely plugged in to the significance of the day. After my meeting, I continued with my day, which included a visit to a nearby Miramar shopping complex in search of a reading lamp for Emilia's apartment. I spent the rest of the morning watching habaneros watch the news. The little furniture store I had been directed to in search of lamps (successfully, as it turned out) set up a TV and a few people were watching, but fewer than I would have expected. There was more going on in the bakery next door, where a radio was announcing Raul's imminent speech and everyone was speaking happily about the release of the Five. Later that day I dropped by Casa de Las Américas, a venerable cultural centre housed in a beautiful Art Deco building at the foot of calle G, overlooking the Malecón. As I'd expected, it was abuzz. TV sets were set up everywhere and everyone was watching. My friends who work there greeted me with hugs and jokes. Gerardo held high his iPad—a prized possession, a gift from a US university colleague. "WiFi on the P1," he declared, referencing a crowded popular bus route. The best Canadian translation for this fantasy scenario might be something like, "Free cocktails on the Spadina bus."

The pattern I saw that day was a mix of optimism and irony, sarcasm and good faith. Ines told me she heard people in her market that afternoon yelling out, "OK, where is the American rice?" As luck would have it, December 17, 2014, fell on a Wednesday, Interactivo's day to perform at el Brecht. So, late that night I gathered there with a group of Cuban and visiting Canadian friends. The Havana Jazz Festival was on and the place was packed. At the table beside us, a group of English speakers, a jazz ensemble from Chicago, started asking us questions about what to expect from Interactivo. Of course, the conversation turned to the announcement that day. "Is this Obama building a legacy?" I asked one of them. "I think it's Obama doing what we fucking elected him to do in the first place," he replied. Then the music started up, and the flamboyant Francis del Rio came on stage with new lyrics to an old song:

Ay Obama, Ay, Obama, vuélvete loco y ven pa' La Habana.
Hey Obama, drive yourself crazy, come to Havana.

It was indeed a great day in Havana. I think the happiest person I spoke to that day was Emilia, a middle-aged woman who trained as an engineer in the Soviet Union—a member of the last Cuban generation to do that. She now works in a Havana clinic. She is a smart, well-educated professional. Some years ago she got to know people from the Center for Democracy in the Americas (CDA), a Washington-based NGO that lobbies for better relations between the US and Cuba. As part of its campaign to get the US government to lift the travel ban and the blockade, the centre basically tries to humanize Cuba for Americans raised on decades of Cold War fear-mongering. It regularly brings delegations of US opinion-makers such as Congress people and journalists to Havana to meet with a wide assortment of people. These visitors meet Havana luminaries such as Carlos Varela, who has for years welcomed a wide swath of American visitors: school children, musicians, and politicians alike. But the CDA also facilitates meetings with "ordinary Cubans" and that is where Emilia comes in. She's become the poster child to show Americans that Cubans do not have horns. For several years, she has received regular invitations from the CDA to events that bring Cubans and visiting Americans together. Sometimes she e-mails me first to give me the list of Congress people whom she is going to meet. I look them up and jokingly recommend those she should avoid and those she should sit next to.

Emilia is the very definition of the active, informed citizen. She cares passionately about her country but is not superficially ideological, and no doubt that's why she keeps getting invited for dinner. A couple of years ago she contacted me with exciting news: instead of bringing Americans to Havana, CDA had invited a number of Cubans to visit Washington for a conference, and she was on the guest list. In order to show off the entrepreneurial spirit of La Nueva Cuba to skeptical Americans, they mostly invited *cuentapropistas*, such as the owners of one of Havana's thriving, high-end restaurants and another who owns a car rental company. Emilia was the only state employee to be invited, of which she and her family were extremely proud. It was her first time in the US, and she was especially excited about a tiny window of opportunity afforded by this invitation. Her travel arrangements permitted her one free day before the conference started, and she wanted to spend it in New York, the city in the world she most wanted to visit. So, one grey November Saturday, Susan Lord and I raced from Kingston to Syracuse, New York, jumped on a train to Manhattan, and spent twenty-seven hours with Emilia in New York City. You can see a surprising amount of New York in twenty-seven hours, and every time we glimpsed an iconic American sight, Emilia peered, looked around, and declared, "I don't see the enemy. Where is the enemy?"

In academic work on foreign policy and international relations, there is a new recognition of what some call "foreign policy from below." Relationships between countries are not made solely by men in business suits who conduct trade relations, declare war or peace, or open embassies. The activities of NGOs like the Center for Democracy in the Americas, and the enthusiastic willingness of people like Emilia or Carlos Varela to be active popular ambassadors, representing not their state but their families, neighbourhoods, and friends, are, I think, where foreign policy is really made. Emilia is no fool and like almost every Cuban I have spoken with, she is skeptical and anxious about what the new relationships with the US will yield. But she is also extremely happy to see her country finally emerge from the Cold War.

A year or so after our whirlwind trip to New York, I was in an IKEA store in Canada and happened to see a huge, framed, black and white photograph, a bird's eye view of Manhattan in the 1960s. I knew just the wall for it, Emilia's apartment on calle Línea. But it took at least six months for me to imagine how I might transport it. It was a more formidable project than even a whole salmon had been. Finally I bought it, and brought it, along with thirty students, on my next Havana trip. It didn't fit on the conveyer belt of the scanner at Pearson airport in Toronto, it almost didn't fit on the airplane, and Havana customs agents looked at me like I was insane when I told them it was simply a photograph, not a huge flat screen TV (which it resembled). But they waved me through and, later that night after the students were settled in the hotel, Susan Lord and Emilia and I made our way down the hill on calle Paseo toward Línea, a little tipsy and laughing like idiots, carrying a huge oversize picture of Manhattan to a Havana apartment.

CONCLUSION

TODO SERÁ DISTINTO?
OUR UNCERTAIN FUTURES

The Havana airport is often a frustrating place, but August 31, 2015, was a low point. I arrived accompanied by Zaira's mother, Maria Teresa, who was returning home from a month-long visit to Canada, her first time out of the country and thus her second time on a plane. As we flew, we skirted around Hurricane Erika, which happily had decided to become Tropical Storm Erika. A nicer version to be sure, but it was a very turbulent flight, which Maria Teresa slept through as I controlled my breathing. As we entered Havana's José Martí airport, already four hours late, it was clear that the bumpy ride was going to continue. It was stiflingly hot. The place overflowed with passengers waiting to claim their luggage. Two huge airplanes full of people were ahead of us, the luggage carousels were immobile, and the waiting passengers looked like zombies. They had obviously been there for a while.

So we settled in. The place came alive about half an hour later as the carousels started up and began their rotation. The deplaned

Iberia passengers cheered as though they were watching the winning goal in a World Cup. That woke everyone up a bit, even those of us who were far behind in the queue. Having arrived at this airport many times, I knew their tricks. Sometimes the luggage appeared as rapidly as one might hope for; other times suitcases trickled in as though from a bad faucet, drop by drop. It seemed pretty clear which phase they were in that night. One carousel would chug forward, another would suddenly stop, and on it went. I tried to amuse myself by people-watching, and was suddenly rewarded for this by the sight of Leonardo Padura among the crowd waiting for the Iberia luggage. Padura is Cuba's foremost novelist, the winner of national and international awards (most recently Spain's Asturias award). Oria, one of my Spanish teachers, had assigned me some of his writing as homework, in order to educate me about literary (rather than street) Spanish. This was a good sighting. He was just as tired and zombie-looking as the rest of us. I pointed him out to Maria Teresa, I exchanged funny texts with friends in Canada, and we all went back to waiting. Thirty minutes later, another tired passenger caught my eye. Could this be Descemer Bueno, Cuba's superstar singer and composer? He's a handsome man, whose signature is a fedora, a look that's easy to imitate. Even though I've seen him perform and have all his CDs, I decided it had to be a look-alike. No one was paying him attention and my head was still running on North American cultural time; superstars don't wait, unrecognized, for hours in inefficient airports for their luggage. I continued to watch as Leonardo Padura approached Descemer Bueno. They recognized each other and embraced. Finally Descemer's luggage trickled out to the carousel, a pilot shook his hand, a few others smiled at him, and off he went. An hour later, so did I, frustrated but still marvelling at this moment of Cuba at its best and worst. One can buy oneself out of many everyday problems in Havana. But sometimes, when things screw up, as they still do very regularly, they screw up for everyone, literary and music stars alike.

As Americans and Canadians—along with a good part of the rest of the world—discuss the possible end of the US blockade and travel ban, Cubans too are trying to wrap their mind around the impact of a potential flood of visitors. Mario Coyula, one of the country's foremost historians of architecture and the author of one of the books I use to teach Canadian students about Havana's history, was recently the subject of a lengthy Al Jazeera interview in which he expressed his grave reservations about how the city could cope with an influx of mass tourism. As someone who has dedicated his professional life to the study of Havana's architecture, Coyula has palpable and understandable fears about the devastation that more tourism to the city could cause.[1] The widely cited statistic offered by Cuba's Ministry of Tourism is that post-US travel ban, Cuba's tourist intake will more than double, from two million to over four million people. That's a lot of suitcases trickling out one at a time.

Yet, after the initial enthusiasm of December 17, 2014, I'd say Cubans have other things on their minds. More than the July 2015 visit of John Kerry to officially open the US embassy, more than the potential lifting of the US blockade and travel ban, what my friends are talking about these days is the weather. Every month of 2015 except one was record-breaking. The heat in Havana in the summer is legendary. Now, summer heat starts in

April or May and continues until at least September. In 2015, Cuba, along with the rest of the Caribbean, suffered a drought. Agricultural production was damaged and at least a million Cubans were relying on trucked-in water for their daily intake. Cuba's National Institute of Water Resources embarked on a public campaign for conservation measures, but the problem is also in the infrastructure. Figures vary but clearly at least some of the problem of scant water in Cuban reservoirs is because of leakage, which matters a lot more when there's no rain.[2] In the winter, the rains now come in intense downpours, causing extensive flooding in Havana and doing little to alleviate the effects of drought in the countryside.

Uruguayan journalist Fernando Ravsburg was for many years the BBC's Cuban correspondent. He still lives in Havana and publishes a regular blog. To my mind he's well-informed, fair-minded, and always worth paying attention to. Like many people on the island, he is trying to put the brakes on wild-eyed predictions of prosperity and plenty that improved relations with the US might produce. Cuba, he says, has gone through two systems, capitalism and socialism, "and has failed at both." Capitalism created wealth in Cuba, but did so "on the basis of brutal inequality," particularly in the countryside. That socialism, too, failed to provide economic prosperity for all is perhaps less a message about the intrinsic goodness or badness of either economic system in the abstract and more an indication that political slogans or labels don't an economy make.[3]

Carlos Varela's ability to put the complexities of economics and politics into poetry helps make sense of Cuba's history, but it also helps me think about the future. "*Todo Será Distinto*"

(Everything will be different) was recorded in 2009 but expresses the conundrum of post-December 17, 2014 Cuba:

> Maybe tomorrow the sun will come out
> And everything will be different
> The sad thing is that then
> We won't be the same.

Those who declare their intentions to visit Cuba now, "before the Americans wreck it," need to take heed of the economic changes that have been occurring in the country for over a decade. American capitalism is hardly the only game in town. Cubans clearly want improvements in many aspects of their lives, above all in their living standards. But what kind of subtle changes in the culture and daily life of Havana are coming? What will become of the city's sense of community and sense of humour, its self-reliance, self-respect, safety, and openness? Its soundtrack? Or the small, everyday acts of generosity, community, and reciprocity that I have come to love. Are these products of socialism, *sociolismo*, or something else? Are these deeply embedded in the culture of daily life, or will they be tossed aside with a "renovated" economic system? The bank I usually go to in Vedado at Linea and Paseo recently installed a screen that counts down numbers for waiting customers. This replaces the person-to-person *ultimo* system, the grassroots line-up that functions for pizza and buses and everything else. The screen-numbering system is modern, efficient, and understandable to everyone, foreigner and Cuban alike. And no one has to talk to anyone.

During a recent visit, Lidice, the mother of two young girls, quizzed me about how my teenage son uses the Internet. She wasn't engaging in Communist paranoia about the tricks of *el enemigo*. She's a highly educated scientist who has studied abroad; she knows the riches the Internet offers. Her concerns were more about whether constant Internet access is isolating for Canadian kids. Does it keep them away from their friends? Does it contribute to or rupture social relations in the neighbourhood or in school? Do people with easy and fast access like me feel the need to control our children's access?

That same visit, the regular meeting of my gay Cerro trade union took place at my house. I prepared couscous that I had brought with me from Canada. I figured it would be considered by my friends to be an exotic alternative to rice, which it was. Omar arrived with a small bag of potatoes for me. They weren't meant as a contribution to dinner. It was more as one might bring a bottle of wine or flowers. He was also thanking me, I think, for the razors and Ibuprofen I brought for him. Potatoes—a prominent feature of the underground economy foreigners are invited into, furtively, in the markets—are a luxury. These days, the harvest has been better, so they are more available and affordable. But their status as a luxury, desired good remains, hence the multiple meanings of Omar's gift. As an outsider—even an intimate one—Cuba's future is not mine to shape. But I think I share the fears and the hopes, in equal measure, of my Cuban friends about what is going to come. I hope, at least, that Havana continues to be the kind of place where old friendships are cemented with potatoes.

NOTES

INTRODUCTION

1. I've heard this story, popular in Cuban studies circles in Canada, attributed to both Professors Hal Klepak and John Kirk. No doubt they would both be honoured to claim credit for it.
2. This list of tourist-sending nations is based on statistics from the first six months of 2015. Venus Carillos Ortega, "Turismo en Cuba," *CubaContemporánea.com* October 26, 2015.
3. Wayne Smith, "Still the Full Moon," *NACLA Report on the Americas* September/October 2004, https://nacla.org; Louis A. Pérez, Jr., "Cuba as an Obsessive Compulsive Disorder," Center for Democracy in the Americas, April 2014, www.democracyinamericas.org.
4. Mélanie Josée Davidson, *Ensalada mixta: geographical explorations of food and Cuba,* MA Thesis, Geography Department, Queen's University, 2015, 64.
5. J.C.M. Ogelsby, *Gringos from the Far North: Essays in the History of Canadian-Latin American Relations, 1866–1968* (Toronto: University of Toronto Press, 1976), 111.
6. Christopher Armstrong and H. V. Nelles, *Southern Exposure: Canadian Promoters in Latin America and the Caribbean, 1896–1930* (Toronto: University of Toronto Press, 1988), 123.

7   Don Munton and David Vogt, "Inside Castro's Cuba: The Revolution and Canada's Embassy in Havana," in Robert Wright and Lana Wylie Wright (eds.), *Our Place in the Sun: Canada and Cuba in the Castro Era* (Toronto: University of Toronto Press, 2009), 46.

8   John W. Graham, *Whose Man in Havana? Adventures from the Far Side of Diplomacy* (Calgary: University of Calgary Press, 2015), 31–52; Don Munton, "Intelligence Cooperation Meets International Studies Theory: Explaining Canadian Operations in Castro's Cuba," *Intelligence and National Security*, 24:1, 2009, 119–138.

9   Cynthia Wright, "Between Nation and Empire: The Fair Play for Cuba Committees and the Making of Canada-Cuba Solidarity in the Early 1960s," in Robert Wright and Lana Wylie Wright, (eds.) *Our Place in the Sun*, 96–120.

10 For more on Sherritt's activities in Cuba, see Rachel Pulfur, "Castro's Favourite Capitalist," *Walrus*, December 2009, and Archibald Ritter, "Canadian-Cuban Economic Relations: Past, Present, and Prospective," in Wright and Wylie Wright, (eds.) *Our Place in the Sun*, 246–281.

11 Rafael Betancourt, "Canadian Universities in Cuba," Report commissioned by the Embassy of Canada in Cuba, 2012.

12 Terry Fox was a young Canadian who, despite losing a leg to cancer, began a cross-country marathon in 1980 to draw attention to cancer research. He died in 1981 and his run has become an annual event.

13 Peter James Hudson, "Imperial Designs: The Royal Bank of Canada in the Caribbean," *Race and Class* Vol. 52.1 Winter 2010, 33–59.

14 "Toronto's Cuba Scene Has Lula Lounge and GTA restaurants including Havana Style Café," *Toronto Star,* July 25, 2015, www.thestar.com.

15 X Alfonso, "Cambiara" *Reverse,* Fabrica de Arte Cubano, 2011.

16 Jennifer Hosek, *Sun, Sex and Socialism: Cuba in the German Imaginary* (Toronto: University of Toronto Press, 2013).

17 Iván de la Nuez, *Fantasía roja Los intelectuales de izquierda y la revolución cubana* (Barcelona: Mondadori, 2006).

18 Moneda Dura, "Tercer mundo" *Alma Sin Bolsillos*, EGREM 2007.

19 Susan Lord, Dannys Montes de Oca Moreda, Zaira Zarza (eds.), "Havana" *Public* 52, Fall 2015.

20 Rachel Weiss, "Some Thoughts on the Right Way (for us) To Love Cuba" in Susan Lord, Dannys Montes de Oca Moreda, Zaira Zarza (eds.) "Havana" *Public* 52, Fall 2015, 49–57.

21 "A Republican Joins Obama in Seeking Ties to Cuba," *New York Times*, February 3, 2015, www.nytimes.com.
22 Molly Kane, "International NGOs and the Aid Industry: Constraints on International Solidarity" *Third World Quarterly* No. 34, Vol. 8, 2013. See also Alisha Nicole Apale and Valerie Stam, *Generation NGO* (Toronto: Between the Lines, 2011), and John S. Saul, *Revolutionary Traveller: Freeze Frames from a Life* (Winnipeg: ARP Books, 2009).

CHAPTER ONE

1 Maria del Carmen Zabala Arguelles, "Poverty and Vulnerability in Cuba Today," in *A Contemporary Cuba Reader,* Second Edition, Philip Brenner et al. (eds.), (Lanham, MD: Rowman and Littlefield, 2015), 173–182.
2 Andrea Carter, "Cuba's Food-Rationing System and Alternatives" in Per Pinstrup-Anderson, "Food Policy for Developing Countries: The Role of Government in the Global Food System," Case Study 4–6, Cornell University, 2011.
3 "Corruption in Cuba: The Cleanup Continues" *The Economist*, Online Edition, May 6, 2011, www.economist.com.
4 Interactivo "A diario," *Goza Pepillo* BIS Music, 2005.
5 "Egg Theft in Havana Leads to 18 Prison Sentences from 5 to 15 Years," *Havana Times,* March 20, 2015, www.havanatimes.org.
6 M. Davidson and C. Krull, "Adapting to Cuba's Shifting Food Landscapes: Women's Strategies of Resistance," *Cuban Studies* Vol. 42, 2011, 59–77.
7 Frank Delgado, "Carta de un niño Cubano a Harry Potter," *Pero, qué dice el coro?* La Lu Produciones, 2008 .
8 Moises Simons, *El Manisero*, New York: E.B.Marks Inc, nd.
9 Vincent Adrisani, "The Sweet Sounds of Havana: Space, Listening and the Making of Sonic Citizenship," *Sounding Out* September 2015 http://soundstudiesblog.com.
10 Maria Magdalena Campos-Pons and Neil Leonard, "*Llego FeFa,*" 11th Havana Biennial 2012, www.google.ca.
11 Ariana Hernandez-Reguant, "Socialism with Commercials: Consuming Advertising in Today's Cuba," *ReVista: Harvard Review of Latin America* Winter 2000. http://revista.drclas.harvard.edu.

12 Silje Lundgren, "'Mami, you're so hot!' Negotiating hierarchies of masculinity through piropos in contemporary Havana," in Laura Alvarez Lopez et al. (eds.), *Stockholm Review of Latin American Studies* 2013, 5–20.
13 Roman de la Campa, *Cuba on My Mind: Journeys to a Severed Nation* (London: Verso, 2000), 41. The most thorough account of Operation Peter Pan remains Maria de los Angeles Torres, *The Lost Apple: Operation Pedro Pan, Cuban Children in the U.S. and the Promise of a Better Future* (Boston: Beacon Press, 2003).
14 Marvin Leiner, *Children are the Revolution: Daycare in Cuba* (New York: Penguin Books, 1974), 131. See also Karen Wald, *Children of Che: Childcare and Education in Cuba* (Palo Alto: Ramparts, 1978).
15 Margot Kirk, "Early Childhood Education in Revolutionary Cuba during the Special Period," in Phillip Brenner et al. (eds.), *A Contemporary Cuba Reader* (New York: Rowman and Littlefield, 2008).
16 "Más círculos infantiles: un problema menos para los padres," *Cubadebate*, February 11, 2015, www.cubadebate.cu.
17 "Crisis con círculos infantiles desestimula crecimiento poblacional en Cuba," *Café Fuerte,* November 9, 2015. http://cafefuerte.com.
18 "Círculos infantiles: cárceles o castillos?" *Diario de Cuba*, April 15, 2015. www.diariodecuba.com.
19 UNICEF, "The Child Care Transition, Innocenti Report Card 8," UNICEF Innocenti Research Centre, Florence, 2008.

CHAPTER TWO

1 John Finn and Chris Luckinbeal, "Musical Cartographies: *Los Ritmos de los Barrios de la Habana"* in Ola Johansson and Thomas Bell, (eds.) *Sound Society and the Geography of Popular Music* (Surrey: Ashgate, 2009), 127–144.
2 I owe this observation to Ruth Warner, from a frustrated text exchange about the general level of ignorance concerning Cuban musical training, in December 2015.
3 This history of musicianship and music education in Cuba draws from Robin D. Moore, *Music and Revolution: Cultural Change in Socialist Cuba* (Berkeley: University of California Press, 2006).
4 Carlos Varela, "Memorias" *Carlos Varela En Vivo* Bis Music 1991.
5 Joaquín Borges-Triana, "Timbatón and the Moral Economy of Perreo," *Cuban Counterpoints,* August 25, 2015, http://cubacounterpoints.com.

6 Geoffrey Baker, *Buena Vista in the Club: Rap, Reggaetón, and Revolution in Havana* (Durham, NC: Duke University Press, 2011).
7 This and subsequent references to Varela's songs are explained more fully in Maria Caridad Cumana, Karen Dubinsky, and Xenia Reloba (eds.), *My Havana: The Musical City of Carlos Varela* (Toronto: University of Toronto Press, 2014).
8 Ana Menéndez, *In Cuba I Was a German Shepherd* (New York: Grove Press, 2001).
9 Carlos Fraguela, "Better than Sex: Cuba's Interactivo," *Havana Times*, January 20, 2015, www.havanatimes.org.
10 *Interactivo, La Pelicula,* Director Tané Martínez (Colorbox Productions, 2011).
11 *Goza Pepillo, Documental,* Directors Ana Maria Rabosa and Cari Rojas (BIS Music, 2006).
12 Ibid.
13 Francis del Rio "No Entiendo Nada," *Interactivo: que lindo es el amor*, RLG Records, 2015.
14 Roberto Carcassés, "Que No Pare El Pare," *Cubanos Por El Mundo,* BIS Music, 2010.
15 *Interactivo, La Pelicula,* Director Tané Martínez (Colorbox Productions, 2011).
16 Fernando Ravsberg, "Un Error no debe conducir a otro Error," Sept. 19, 2013, www.bbc.co.uk.
17 Susan Thomas, "Did No One Pass the Girls the Guitar? Queer Appropriations in Cuban Popular Song," *Journal of Popular Music Studies* vol. 18, no. 2 (2006), 124–143.
18 Telmary "Que Equivoca'o," *A Diario*, BIS Music, 2007.
19 Kalamu ya Salaam, "Review: Telmary Diaz "Que Equivoca'o," *The New Black Magazine,* Friday, November 9, 2007, www.thenewblackmagazine.com.
20 "Rochy," *Ecudred.cu* No date. http://www.ecured.cu. Julio César explains the anti-violence against women campaign in Cuba in detail (in English translation) in an interview: Karen Dubinsky, Julio César González Pagés, Anne Rubenstein, Michael Kaufman & Zaira Zarza, "'Masculinities in Latin America and beyond': a panel discussion with Julio César González Pagés, Anne Rubenstein, and Michael Kaufman." *Canadian Journal of Latin American and Caribbean Studies/Revue canadiennedes études latino-américaines et caraïbes*, 39:1, (2014), 139–156.

21 Patricia Grogg, "Violence Against Women Out of the Closet," Interpress News Agency, November 27, 2011. www.ipsnews.net.
22 "Rochy Ameniero, cantante cubana y líder del proyecto cultural Todas Contracorriente," *Cubainformacíon,* June 19, 2013, www.cubainformacion.tv.
23 "Suzanne Cope, "The New Face of Havana Nightlife," *Punchdrunk,* June 25, 2015, http://punchdrink.com.
24 Laura Evans, "Havana Nights: Where to Party in Cuba" *Gothamist,* July 6, 2015, http://gothamist.com.
25 X Alfonso, "Mi Abuelo Dice," *Interactivo que lindo es el amor,* RLG Records, 2015.
26 X Alfonso, "Revoluxcion," *Revoluxcion* National, 2011.

CHAPTER THREE

1 Jeffrey Goldberg, "Fidel: 'Cuban Model Doesn't Even Work for Us Anymore,'" *The Atlantic,* September 8, 2010, www.theatlantic.com.
2 Jorge Mario Sánchez Egozcue, "Challenges of Economic Restructuring in Cuba," in Philip Brenner, Marguerite Rose Jiménez, John M. Kirk, William M. Leogrande, *A Contemporary Cuba Reader,* Second Edition (Lanham, MD: Rowman and Littlefield, 2015), 129.
3 Ibid. See also Philip Peters, "Cuba's Entrepreneurs: Foundation of a New Private Sector," in Phillip Brenner et al., 145–153.
4 Richard E. Feinberg, *Soft Landing in Cuba? Emerging Entrepreneurs and Middle Classes,* Latin American Initiatives at Brookings, November 2013.
5 Ibid, 34.
6 "An Arugula Growing Farmer Feeds a Culinary Revolution in Cuba," *Washington Post.com,* August 21, 2015, www.washingtonpost.com.
7 "Cubans Are Confident USA Will Alleviate Their Suffering," *Havana Times,* February 5, 2015, www.havanatimes.org.
8 Thomas J. Donohue, "We Applaud and Support Your Reforms," *Progresso Weekly,* May 29, 2014, http://progressoweekly.us.
9 "Cuba's President Raúl Castro's speech at the close of Cuba's National Assembly session," December 18, 2010, Voltaire.net.org, www.voltairenet.org.
10 Pedro Monreal, "La globalización y los dilemas de las trayectorias económicas de Cuba," *Temas* 30, Septiembre 2002, 4.
11 *The Technological Disobediance of Ernesto Oroza,* Motherboard Films, 2013, www.youtube.com.

12. http://havana-cultura.com.
13. "Gallo's World," *Cuba Absolutely,* www.cubaabsolutely.com.
14. Philip Peters, *Cuba's Real Estate Market* (Washington: Brookings Institute, February 2014), 1.
15. Hope Bastian Martinez, "Housing in Havana," *Anthropology News,* November 2013, www.anthropology-news.org.
16. Carollee Bengelsdorf, *The Problem of Democracy in Cuba: Between Vision and Reality* (New York: Oxford University Press, 1994), 179.
17. "Batallón de policías sale a recoger basura en La Habana," *Café Fuerte,* http://cafefuerte.com.
18. Yusnaby Post, July 15, 2015, http://yusnaby.com.
19. Geoffrey Baker, *Buena Vista in the Club: Rap, Reggaetón and Revolution in Havana* (Durham, NC: Duke University Press, 2011), 223.
20. "Cuba: un juicio cada tres minutos en tribunal," *Café Fuerte,* July 5, 2014, http://cafefuerte.com.
21. Dick Cluster, "To Live Outside the Law You Must be Honest," in *Cuba Today: Continuity and Change since the "Periodo Especial,"* in Mauricio Font (ed.), *Visions of Power in Cuba* (New York: Bildner Center for Western Hemisphere Studies, 2005), 31–40.
22. Kabir Vega Castellanos, "Time Has No Value in Cuba," *Havana Times,* July 30, 2015, www.havanatimes.org.
23. Circles Robinson, "Cuba Sends 6 Teachers to Jail for Academic Fraud," *Havana Times,* November 4, 2014, www.havanatimes.org.
24. "Atlanta Educators Convicted in School Cheating Scandal," *New York Times.com,* April 1, 2015, www.nytimes.com.
25. "Art Theft in Havana," *Cuba Art News,* March 4, 2014, www.cubanartnews.org.
26. "Cuban poison moonshine defendants get sentences of up to 30 years," *The Guardian,* June 18, 2014,www.theguardian.com.
27. "Shock at Deaths and Corruption in Psychiatric Hospital," Inter Press Service, January 25, 2011, www.ipsnews.net.
28. Morales' blog is at http://estebanmoralesdominguez.blogspot.ca His article on corruption is reprinted in a collection of his writings, *El Reto de Mirar Hacia Adentro* (The Challenge of Looking Inside) (Coral Gables, FL: Editorial Letra Viva, 2014).
29. "Esteban Morales on 'Corrosive' Corruption in Cuba," *Havana Times,* August 19, 2010, www.havanatimes.org.

30 Joseph L. Scarpaci, Roberto Segre, and Mario Coyula, *Havana: Two Faces of the Antillean Metropolis,* Revised Edition (Chapel Hill: University of North Carolina Press, 2002).
31 "Sixty Havana Waste Management Employees Accused of Corruption," *Havana Times,* November 26, 2014, www.havanatimes.org.
32 "Batallón de policías sale a recoger basura en La Habana," *Café Fuerte,* January 6, 2015, http://cafefuerte.com.

CHAPTER FOUR

1 "Measuring the Information Society Report 2014," www.itu.int (International Telecommunications Union, Geneva Switzerland, 2014), 58, 102, 103. See also Jorge Domínquez, "What you might not know about the Cuban economy," *Harvard Business Review,* August 17, 2015, https://hbr.org.
2 John M. Kirk, "Surfing Revolico.com, Cuba's Answer to Craig's List," in Phillip Brenner et al. (eds.), *A Contemporary Cuba Reader,* Second Edition. 443–446.
3 www.havanastreetview.com.
4 "The world in a package," *Progreso Semanal,* April 3, 2014.
5 "No Internet? No Problem," *Forbes* Magazine, July 1, 2015.
6 Frank Delgado, "La Otra Orilla," *La Habana Está de bala,* BIS Music, 1998.

CONCLUSION

1 "Does the Diplomatic Thaw Mean the End of Old Havana?" Al Jazeera, July 18, 2015, www.aljazeera.com.
2 "Cuba on Edge as Drought Worsens," Reuters.com, August 17, 2015, www.reuters.com.
3 Fernando Ravsburg, "Cuba's Problems Cannot Be Solved With Magic Spells," *Cartes Desde Cuba,* August 27, 2015, http://cartasdesdecuba.com.

INDEX

[Note: page numbers in italics refer to images]

Adichie, Chimamanda Ngozi, 23
Adrisani, Vincent, 47
advertisements, 47, 50
agromercado (market), 35–36
Aitkin, Max (Lord Beaverbrook), 11
alcohol poisoning scandal, 147–48
Alfonso, Carlos, 107
Alfonso, Eme, 107
Alfonso, Gerardo, 92, 95
Alfonso, X, 19, 106–12; "*Mi Abuelo Dice*" [My Grandfather Says], 108; "*Revoluxcion*," 112
Allende, Salvador, 38
Almodóvar, Pedro, 25
Ameneiro, Rochy, 97, 102–4
Anti-Imperialist Tribunal (*protestodromo*), 4, 88
apartment matching, 31
Arafat, Yasser, 22

Bajo el mismo sol [Under the Same Sun], 103
Baker, Geoffrey, 77
Bank of Nova Scotia, *14–15*, 16
Baraka, Amiri, 20
Barreto: "*Viente Años*" [Twenty Years], 73
baseball, 51–52
Bastian Martinez, Hope, 128–30
Batista, Fulgencio, 11, 17
Bay of Pigs invasion, 61
Belafonte, Harry, 77
Beltrán, Marcel, 168
Belyea, Susan, 5, 36, 44, 54, 91, 105
Belyea Dubinsky, Jordi, 6, 62, 64, 105, 162, 168–70, 182
Beyoncé, 2, 170
bicycles, 42
Bieber, Justin, 16

★ 193

bodegas, 36, 39
Bolívar, Simón, 68
Borges-Triana, Joaquín, 16, 26, 76–77, 91, 92, 164, 166–67
brand consciousness, 118
Browne, Jackson, 81
Bryans, Billy, 99
Buena Vista Social Club, 97
Bueno, Descemer, 26, 178–79
Bunnett, Jane, 99
Bush, George W., 4

Café Madrigal, 121
cakes, 42–44
Callejon de Hamel, 126–27
Campos-Pons, Maria Magdalena, 47
Canada: Cuban diaspora in, 18; cultural influences on Cuba, 16–17; diplomatic ties with Cuba, 11–12; economic ties with Cuba, 13; items purchased in for Cubans, 162–64, 167; as tourist-sending nation, 1
Canción de Barrio [Neighbourhood Song], 135–36
capitalism, 3, 124, 158, 180–81
Carballea, Enrique, 84
Carcassés, Bobby, 83
Carcassés, Roberto, 83–85, 89 90; "*Que no pare el Pure*," 88
Carpentier, Alejo, 149
cars, 114, 115, 118, 125, 138
Casa de Las Américas, 172–73
casas de cultura, 75
Castro, Fidel, 8, 12, 19, 30, 61, 63, 77–78, 90, 113, 138, 142, 172

Castro, Mariela, 54
Castro, Raúl, 1, 8–9, 113, 121, 123, 124, 172
celebrity culture, 82, 95–96
cellphones, 155, 157, 159
censorship, 75–76, 79, 90, 112
Center for Democracy in the Americas (CDA), 174–75
Centro Pablo Press, 90
Centro Vocacional de Lenin, 69
Cerro, 51–56, 128, 155, 182
children/childhood, 60–71; lack of consumer culture, 114–15
CIDA exchange programs, 13
Cienfuegos, Camilo, 68
Circulos Infantiles. *See* daycares
Cluster, Dick: "To Live Outside the Law You Must be Honest," 143
Cold War, 4, 11, 85, 138, 174–75
Cole, Teju, 23
Colome, Abelardo, 121
Colome, Jose, 121
communications system, 154–60
communism, 3, 75; "hippie," 92, 95–96
consumer economy: lack of, 160; underground, 162
corruption, 144–49, 152
Costco, taking Cubans to, 164–68
Coyula, Mario, 179
crime, 102, 105, 142–46; armed robbery, 143
Cruz, Celia, 75, 97
Cuban controvertible peso (CUC), 8, 33–34, 36, 109, 130
Cuban Federation of Women (FMC), 65

"Cuban Five" (Los Cinco Heroes), 88, 172
Cubanidad [Cubanness], 136
"Cuban missile crisis," 8, 12
Cuban Music Institute, 89, 94
Cuban pesos. *See moneda nacional*
Cuban Railroad Company, 10
Cuban revolution (1959), 11, 60, 69, 74, 79, 80, 138
cuentapropismo (self-employment), 9, 29, 70, 114, 117–18, 131, 143, 175
cultural mixing, 73
Cumaná, Caridad, 78, 82, 139
currency system, 8, 127

Davidson, Melanie, 40
Davis, Angela, 20
daycares, 61, 63–71
de Beauvoir, Simone, 19–20
D17 (December 17, 2014), 1–2, 6, 9, 11, 32, 96, 107, 114, 170–73, 179, 181
"decolonized cosmopolitanism," 20
de la Campa, Ramón, 61
de la Nuez, Iván, 19–20; *Fantasía Rojo* [Red Fantasy], 19–20
Delany, Ian, 13
Delgado, Frank, 85, 92, 96; "A Letter from a Cuban Child to Harry Potter," 40; "*La Otra Orilla*" [The Other Shore], 166
del Rio, Francis, 93, 85, 173
Díaz, Jesus, 166
Díaz, Telmary, 38, 83–85, 97–101, 119; *A Diario*, 98; "Music is My Weapon," 106; "*Que Equivoca'o*," 98
Diefenbaker, John, 12

Dion, Céline, 16
Donohue, Thomas J., 123
drought, 180
Dubinsky, Karen, *111*
Dylan, Bob, 94–95, 143

eastern Cuba, 170–71
economic transformation, 8–9, 55, 113–53, 181
economy: black market, 115; formal vs. informal, 37; new, 113–53; underground, 114, 143, 162
El Brecht (Bertolt Brecht Cultural Centre), 82–90, 173
El Calde: "*Se Calentó*," 104–5
energy conservation, 126
entrepreneurship, 27, 31, 38, 56, 117, 123, 125, 127, 156, 158–59, 174–75
ETECSA (telephone company), 55, 155, 157, 159

Fábrica de Arte Cubano (FAC), 94, 106–12
"Fair Play for Cuba" groups, 12
Feinberg, Richard, 117–18
Feliú, Santiago, 90–96, 112; "*Para Barbara*" [For Barbara], 96
femininity, 54, 97
feminism, 57–59, 99
Fernández, Darsi, 83
Flake, Jeff, 22
food, 3–42, 119–23; food stands, 115–17
Fowler, Victor, 158
Fox, Terry, 16
Free Hole Negro, 99

Fuente, La, 120
Futuros Communistas daycare, 65, 66, 69

Galeano, Eduardo, 18
Gallo, Hector Pasual: "Garden of Affections," 127
Gandhi, Leela, 23
garage bands, 74
garbage, 149–53
García, Josué, 91, 112
gay community, 53–55, 182
Gema and Pavel: "*Helado Sobre Ruedas*" [Ice Cream on Wheels], 47
Gente de Zona (group), 26, 105–6
Gitlin, Todd, 20
Goldberg, Jeffrey, 113
González, Elián, 61–63
González Pagés, Julio César, 58, 93, 102, *103*, 104, 189n20
Graham, John W., 12
Granma, 4
Grant, Cary, 46–47
Gross, Allan, 172
"*Guantanamera*," 75
Guatemala, 105
Guevara, Che, 4, 19–20, 30, 68

Habana Blues, 156
Havana, 23–27, airport, 177–79; as beautiful, wounded city, 3; freedom of movement in, 7; as "Paris of the Caribbean," 3; Pride Day, 54; real estate in, 127–38; restaurants in, 119–23; sound of, 72–112; symbolic Canadianization of, 17
Havana Biennial, 45–46, 126
Havana Book Fair (Feria del Libro), 90
Havana International Film Festival, 32
Havana Jazz Festival, 74, 173
Havana Psychiatric Hospital, 147–48
"Havana Street View," 158
Hevia, Liuba María, 64
hip hop, 77–78, 98
Ho Chi Minh, 22
homophobia, 55, 97
Hosek, Jennifer, 19
housing problem, 132–38
Human Poverty Index, 34
Humbertico, Papá, 141
hypersexuality, 77

ideology, 4, 7, 23–25, 47, 132
Iglesias, Enrique, 26
immigration, 79
Industriales (baseball team), 52
inequality: global, 24, 62; racial, 8, 34
Infomed, 156
Instituto de Farmacia y Alimentos, 147
Instituto Superior del Arte (ISA), 92, 109
Interactivo, 74, 82–90, 97, 99, 108, 173; "*Cubanos por el mundo*," 88
International Children's Day, 63
International Telecommunications Union, 154–55
International Women's Day, 59
Internet, 154–60, 182

Jay-Z, 2, 107, 170

Kane, Molly, 23
Kennedy, John F., 12
Kerry, John, 179
kiosk economy, 116–17, 158
Kirk, John, 185n1
Klepak, Hal, 185n1
Krull, Cathy, 40

Labatt brewers, 13
Laferrière, Dany, 23
land line service, 155–57
Las PePe, 121
left intelligentsia, Western: fascination of with Cuba, 20
legality/illegality, 143–44
Lejania, 166
Lenin, Vladimir, 80
Lennon, John, 20
Leonard, Neil, 47
lesbian and gay rights, 54
libreta system (*Libreta de Abastecimientos*), 36–38
Litoral, El, 120–21
Lopez, Elio Hector, 159
Lord, Susan, 20, 82, *111*, 121
Los Aldeanos, 84
lucha, la, 127
Luxemburg, Rosa, 68

maniseras/maniseros, 50–51
maquinas, 139–40
Martí, José, 4, 68
masculinity, 58, 97, 102
masturbation, public, 25, 58

McTurk, James, 16
men, 56–60
Menéndez, Ana: "In Cuba I was a German Shepherd," 81
Mexico, 11
"micros," 132
middle class, 25, 114, 119
Mills, C. Wright, 20
Monasterio Barsó, Freddy, 112
Moneda Dura: "*Tercer Mundo*" [Third World], 20
moneda nacional (MN; Cuban pesos), 8, 34, 35–36, 109, 116, 130
Monreal, Pedro, 125
"Monstruos devoradores de Energia" [Energy Devouring Monsters], 126
Morales, Esteban, 148–49
Mother's Day, 58–59, 158
Museo de Bellas Artes, 147
music, 72–112, 170; and history, 78–82; income from, 85; misogyny of, 104; and women, 84, 97–106

Nasatir, Robert, 91
National Institute of Water Resources, 180
Nauta program, 157
neo-liberalism, 124
new economy, 113–53
normalcy, 166–67
"Nueva Trova," 91–92, 108
Nuñez, Pastorita, 52

Obama, Barack, 1–2, 22, 32, 88, 97, 138, 172–73
O'Brien, Conan, 2

Old Havana, 29, 50–51, 54, 55, 73, 84, 91, 120, 128, 134, 137, 161
Only Angels Have Wings, 46–47
Operation Peter Pan, 60–61, 63
"Oriente." *See* eastern Cuba
Oroza, Ernesto, 125
over-consumption, 165, 167
overcrowding, 132–33

Pabexpo Exhibition Complex, 161
Padura, Leonardo, 178
panaderías, 36, 39
Pánfilo, 44–46
el Paquete Semanal, 158–59, 170
Parkins, David, 2, *3*
Pastors for Peace, 70
Paz, Mary, 84
Pérez, Louis, 4; *On Becoming Cuban*, 16
permuta system, 128, 133
Perugorría, Jorge, 129
Polzot, Christina, 171–72
Portuanda, Omara, 97, 134–35
potatoes, 35, 182
poverty, 34, 99, 134–36
pregoneros, 46–51
Prieto, Elio: "Travels by Taxi," 138
private sector, 118. *See also* new economy
"Proposed Guidelines of the Economic and Social Policy," 113
protestodromo (Anti-Imperialist Tribunal), 4, 88

racism, 45, 148
Ramírez Anderson, Alejandro, 134–36

Ravsburg, Fernando, 180
real estate, 114, 127–38
recycling, 150, *151*
reggaetón, 76–77, 104
Reloba, Xenia, 22, 90–91, 95, 154, 164–65
resourcefulness, 125, 127
restaurants, 119–23, 175
Rio Zaza, 39
Rochy. *See under* Ameneiro, Rochy
Rodríguez, Ines, 170–71
Rodríguez, Silvio, 76, 78, 89–90, 134–36
Rosenberg, Ethel, 20, *21*, 22
Rosenberg, Julius, 20, *21*, 22
Royal Bank of Canada, 16–17

Sánchez, Celia, 68
Sánchez, Jorge Mario, 114, 120
Sands, Bobby, 22
Santa, Melvis, 88
Santaria, 18
Sartre, Jean-Paul, 19–20
self-employment. *See cuentapropismo*
Se Permuta, 128
Se Vende, 129
sexism, 77, 97, 102
Sherritt International, 13
shopping, 160–68
"The Shopping," 33, 35
Simons, Moisés: "*El Manisero*" [The Peanut Vendor], 46–47
Síntesis, 107–8
Smith, Wayne, 4
socialism, 7, 46, 124, 146, 180–81

sociolismo, 38, 181; vs. *socialismo*, 7, 146
Solaya, Marilyn, 24–25; *Vestido de Novia* [His Wedding Dress], 25, 103
Sontag, Susan, 20
Sosa, Mercedes, 32
Soviet Union, 8, 39, 61; collapse of, 80
"Special Period," 8, 39–40, 43, 51, 65, 125, 127
Springsteen, Bruce, 78
StarBien, 121, *123*
stereotypes, 4–5, 17–18, 22, 54, 102, 154
Super Burger, 121, *122–23*
syncretism, 73

taxis, 138–41
"technological disobedience," 126–27, 158
Telmary. *See under* Díaz, Telmary
Thomas, Susan: "Did Nobody Pass the Girls the Guitar?," 97
Those Who Dream with Their Ears, 26
Tienda de Los Rusos, La, 118–19
"*Todas Contracorriente*," 102
tourism, 1–2, 58, 96, 107, 124; incentives for, 8; influx of, 179; mocking of, 19–20, 141–42; preference for Germans over Canadians, 5
transgender rights, 54
trova, 97, 102
Trudeau, Margaret, 12–13
Trudeau, Pierre, 12
Tzara, Tristan, 80

ultimo system, 60, 181
UNICEF, 71
United Nations Millennium Development Goals, 34
United States: absence from Cuba, 2; animosity toward Cuba, 2; cultural influences, 16; economic blockade of Cuba, 37, 79, 125, 174, 179; embassy in Havana, 3–4, 12, 179; relationship with Cuba, 10, 32, 174. *See also* D17 (December 17, 2014)
utility costs, 31

Valdés, Ele, 107
Valdés, Oliver, 83
Van Horne, William, 10–11
Varela, Carlos, 76, 78–82, 84, 90–92, 94–96, *110*, 143, 164, 174–75, 180; "Backdrop," 80–81; "Checkmate 1916," 80; "Everyone Steals," 81; "Hanging from the Sky," 80–81; "*Memorias*," 76; "Now That the Maps Are Changing Colour," 80; "Politics Don't Fit in a Sugar Bowl," 79–80; "Robinson," 80; "The Sons of William Tell," 79; "*Todo Será Distinto*," 180–81; "*Todo se roban*," 144–45; "The Woodcutter without a Forest," 81
Vedado, 29–31, 33, 51, 55, 73–74, 83, 86–87, 99, 118, 121, 130, 134, 141, 161
violence, 102–5, 142; against women, 102, 189n20

Walmart, 165, 167
Warner, 188n2
War on Terror, 4
weather, 179–80
Weiss, Rachel, 22
West, Kanye, 170
Wickery, Stephen, 172
wine, 118–19
women, 56–60; and independence, 103; and music, 84, 97–106; *piropos* vs. *groseros*, 57–58; predominance of in markets, 39–40; violence against, 189n20
World Festival of Youth and Students, 18–19

"Yo Digo No" ("I Say No") anti-violence campaign, *103*, 105
"Your Freedom" program, 157
Yusa, 83

ABOUT THE AUTHOR

Karen Dubinsky has observed Havana and Cuba as an intimate outsider for many years. She regularly brings university students from Canada to Havana to learn about Cuban economic and cultural development, and she hosts Cuban musicians and academics in Canada. She has written about legendary Cuban musician Carlos Varela in *My Havana: The Musical City of Carlos Varela*, and on Cuban child migration conflicts in *Babies Without Borders: Adoption and Migration Conflicts Across the Americas*. Her other books include *The Second Greatest Disappointment: Honeymooning and Tourism at Niagara Falls*, and *New World Coming: The Sixties and the Shaping of Global Consciousness*. She teaches in the departments of Global Development Studies and History at Queen's University in Kingston, Ontario.

Shelfie

An **ebook** edition is available for $2.99 with the purchase of this print book.

CLEARLY PRINT YOUR NAME ABOVE IN UPPER CASE

Instructions to claim your eBook edition:
1. Download the Shelfie app for Android or iOS
2. Write your name in **UPPER CASE** above
3. Use the Shelfie app to submit a photo
4. Download your eBook to any device

ISBN 978-1-77113-269-5